Revival!

Revival!

By

Richard Owen Roberts

Richard Owen Roberts, Publishers
Wheaton, Illinois
1997

RICHARD OWEN ROBERTS, PUBLISHERS
Post Office Box 21
Wheaton, Illinois 60189 U.S.A.

First edition, August 1982
Second Printing, December 1983
Third Printing, May 1985
Fourth Printing, May 1986
Fifth Printing, March 1988
Second edition, March 1991
Second Printing , August 1993
Third Printing, March 1997

Printed in the United States of America

ISBN 0-940033-36-4

Library of Congress
Catalogue Card No. 82-60247

All Scripture references unless otherwise noted are from
the King James version of the Bible.

To my parents
whose love,
spiritual concern,
and prayers
have been
of unceasing help.

Contents

Introduction

"Why are we here?" Isn't this one of the greatest questions we could possibly ask?

A thoughtful look at the Western world would reveal that a vast number of people have decided they are here to enjoy themselves. The pursuit of pleasure in all its varied forms is mankind's current obsession. The old adage, "Eat, drink, and be merry, for tomorrow ye die," is contemporary enough to be written tomorrow morning. If we can believe our peers, marriage is for pleasure, work is for pleasure, food and drink are for pleasure, bodies are for pleasure, time is for pleasure, as are health, strength, opportunity and wealth.

Whatever is not pleasurable is to be ruthlessly eliminated; whatever is pleasurable is to be grasped at any cost. By this zany view of life the only laws that must be ultimately yielded to are the laws of self-gratification and self-preservation. Any other laws are made to bend before the supreme law of personal pleasure. Thus, the ancient moral laws handed down on Mount Sinai are now considered absurdly out of date. Forms of conduct written into the very foundations of our society are contemptuously treated as idiotic mores designed by puritanical tyrants to rob men of their rightful pleasures.

But, are we, in fact, here to enjoy ourselves? Is personal pleasure man's chief end?

In their Shorter Catechism, the Westminster divines asked, "What is the chief end of man?" With absolute accuracy and splendid conciseness they answered, "Man's chief end is to glorify God, and to enjoy Him forever." Any pursuit of pleasure apart from God who made us is a violation of God's purpose in the creation of man and a travesty against man's own best interests. Man was not made for himself but for God. To pursue self-gratification to the abandonment of God's creative purpose is to guarantee both immediate disappointment and eventual total ruin. That is not to say pleasure cannot be found apart from God. There is indeed pleasure in sin, but the fleeting nature of pleasures and the rapidity with which they take flight promise future disappointment, while the violation of the plan and purpose of God in the creation of man guarantees ultimate ruin.

The greatest need of this generation is a wholehearted return to the plan and purpose of God. What can bring men back to this plan and purpose? Can the Church, as it is now functioning? Can government? Can new laws? Can education? Can social and moral improvement endeavors? Or is the world so hopelessly befuddled that it can only get worse and worse?

This book has grown out of the profound conviction that *revival* is the only answer. Revival will bring great masses of people to their senses and to God. Can anything else? Men in their current state will not glorify God, nor can they. Can you conceive of anything that might happen which could possibly do as much to enable men to glorify God as a genuine revival? I certainly cannot!

There is absolutely no question in my mind that a revived people will glorify God in a way they cannot glorify Him in their backsliding. When men and women learn to glorify God, they can really begin to enjoy Him. Their enjoyment will not be seasonal but eternal. When God is glorified and enjoyed, the mad pursuit of temporary pleasures is abandoned with enthusiasm and thanksgiving. What was once an inconceivable drudgery and restriction of the free spirit of man will become pure freedom and pleasure. What was previously sheer enjoyment will become filthy and depraved conduct more appropriate to the vile denizens of hell than to noble citizens of earth created in the image of God.

What is revival? When is revival needed? When can it be expected? What truth must it emphasize? What are the dangers of revival? What are the hindrances to revival? Will the fruits of revival last? These are the questions I urge upon your consideration.

Some thirty years ago, while doing library research in London, I was unwisely and inaccurately introduced to a British scholar as "an American expert on revivals." His pleasant, but sharp, retort was unforgettable: "Knowing everything there is to know about revivals will not produce one." Desiring to respond in kind, I countered, "Neither will ignorance." The truth of both these remarks stands today—neither knowledge about revivals nor ignorance concerning them will produce the gracious outpouring of divine blessing so greatly needed at this time.

Rather than writing merely to inform and to overcome revival ignorance, I have written with the conviction that the *experience* of revival is worth far more than facts concerning it, no matter how consequential that information may be. I therefore urge you to read this book, not so much for the information it contains, as for the effect its truths can have upon your life. Read it with a tender heart, an open mind and a questing spirit. Read it with an ever increasing fervency in praying, "Oh, God, wilt Thou not revive us again that Thy people may rejoice in Thee?"

When the first edition of this volume appeared in 1982 I indicated my firm conviction that revival was coming and expressed fervent hope this volume would assist many in preparing for that marvelous visitation of divine grace I anticipated.

Now eight years later I am even more convinced that revival is on the way. The need for it has increased horrendously. The burden for awakening among both pastors and people has grown considerably over these years and continues to mount up with increasing numbers and fervency. The growth of the prayer movement, especially in massive Concerts of Prayer, appears to be a certain portent of good. For one man to get other men to pray once or twice about a matter of deep spiritual concern is a very difficult task. To keep them praying fervently, with tears and groanings is impossible. And yet this is exactly what is happening. Only God could have caused it. And surely he would not have stirred so many to fasting and prayer only to later laugh and say, "I just wanted to see if you would do it." No! God has stirred His people to pray because He intends to quicken them once again!

And what about the Solemn Assemblies that are being called? Is not this biblical response of repentance from corporate sin exactly what the Father demands? And are they not also heart-warming signs of God's intentions for His people when they are truly broken and contrite before Him?

This is not to say that the response of the Church to her Lord has been adequate. God Himself is the judge of that. But it is to call for rejoicing for increasing evidences of the hand of God at work among His people.

Oh, for the day when the Lord will rend the heavens and come down. Oh, for the time when He will make bare His mighty arm. Oh, for the season when grace once again flows like a mighty river and the glory of the Lord fills the earth. Do it again, Lord! Do it again!

Richard Owen Roberts
February 1991

Chapter One

What

Is

Revival?

The sea is out and I cannot bring a wind and cause it to flow again: only I wait on the shore till the Lord sends a full sea.

Samuel Rutherford, St. Andrews, Scotland

We look at some mighty estuary which the retiring tide has left bare of the water. We see a vast expanse of sand and mud, with little trickling rivulets wearing their scarcely appreciable way through the resisting banks of that yielding ooze: and the many who know not the secrets of the tide and the influence by which God governs nature would say, "How can you ever expect to see that great expanse covered? Look at those sandbanks, those mud-heaps; how by any contrivance are you to cover them? You had better give up the thought and acquiesce in the perpetual sterility and enduring ooze." But high in the heavens, the unseen Ruler has set the orb which shall bring in her time the tides of the surrounding ocean, and when the appointed moment comes, noiselessly and unobserved, but suddenly and sufficiently, the whole is covered by the rejoicing water, and again it is one argent surface, sandless and mudless, because the Lord hath willed it.

Bishop Wilberforce, Winchester, England

What Is Revival?

What is *revival*? A series of special meetings? An emotional religious extravaganza? Loud music and thunderous hell-fire preaching? A chapter from the wisely forgotten past? A quickly passing spiritual phenomenon? A deep and vital transformation of society initiated by the Spirit of God?

Is it not immediately apparent that in using the term *revival* one runs the risk of being misunderstood? What revival means to a Southerner may be very different from what a Northeasterner has in mind. A European's concept of revival may be altogether different from that of an American.

If a precise definition of revival were provided, it probably would not be possible to get everyone to accept it. Having been used in a number of different ways over a long period of years, the word *revival* may now actually mean a variety of things.

Therefore, without regard to what others mean when they speak of revival, let me clearly state what I am talking about. If I ask you to agree with my definition of revival you may find it difficult, but if I ask you to understand my use of the term, you can then think with me on this grand and vital subject.

Let me begin by declaring what I am not talking about. By *revival* I do not mean scheduled meetings. In many parts of America it is common to hold *"revivals"*. One frequently sees signs announcing: *Revival— One Week Only* or *Revival Every Night Except Saturday*. These signs indicate that special meetings are being held. The sponsors and the participants may well believe they are conducting a revival, but I am not using the term to describe any meetings which man can schedule or conduct at his own volition. Even if the scheduled meetings become popular and crowded and result in much interest, I am still not ready to describe this as revival.

When the term *revival* is applied to organized mass evangelism, both concepts suffer. As significant as mass evangelism is, and as wise as it may be to organize this work carefully—such labors cannot be called *revival* with any degree of accuracy. Mass evangelism is work men do for Christ. *Revival* is something Christ does for men.

By *revival* I certainly do not mean an emotional extravaganza. According to certain sociologists, revival is indeed an orgy of emotions. Amazing tales are told of camp meetings and frontier movements where revival subjects barked up trees like dogs after possum and cracked their long hair like whips when taken with the *jerks*. If such things actually happened, they had little or nothing to do with genuine revival. I decline to use the term *revival* to describe foolishness, fanaticism, and other human evidences of depravity. I also dismiss cleverly calculated efforts at the manipulation of men's minds in order to produce a desired religious response. Meetings of this type have sometimes been called *revivals*.

Even church growth—a subject of much concern to Christian workers and doubtless to Christ—is not what I have in mind when using the term revival. Many churches, following carefully laid out biblical principles, are seeing consistent and exciting growth. However, if we make church growth synonymous with revival, we will miss something of the wonder and reality of the greater work God is able to perform.

In using the term *revival*, I am speaking of *an extraordinary movement of the Holy Spirit producing extraordinary results*. Let me illustrate by describing three ordinary approaches to preaching and the expected results of each.

THREE COMMON TYPES OF PREACHING

Mouth-to-ear preaching. In the preparation of sermons some men are greatly concerned with the choice and organization of their words. Their chief goal, apparently, is to speak well and to sound good. The words from the mouth of the preacher enter the ears of the hearers and produce the expected or ordinary results. Such preaching is not generally calculated to produce conviction of sin or to inspire men to repentance—and it usually does neither. It may provoke comments like, "What a lovely sermon. I really enjoyed it!" or "I love the way you make us feel when you preach!" or even such inane statements as "Beautiful day, isn't it?" If mouth-to-ear preaching resulted in a general feeling of alarm among the congregation, it would be truly extraordinary. No one would be more surprised than the preacher himself.

Head-to-head preaching. Some preachers are very thoughtful and studious and give careful attention to the contents of their sermons. When they preach, they desire to stimulate thinking and affect the minds of their listeners. They expect to teach some important truth, be it humanitarian, moral, or religious; they anticipate that at least some of their congregation will learn from the experience. If the head-to-head preacher hears only comments about the latest sporting event following his sermon, he may well wonder what happened to the ordinary results of ordinary preaching. This preacher has every reason to expect that at least part of his congregation will have their minds attuned to his mind and will receive some new understanding or insight as the result of his efforts. He may wisely anticipate such remarks as, "That was a great sermon. I never thought of it like that before!" or "You really got me thinking this time, Pastor!"

Soul-to-soul preaching. Some preachers are deeply involved in the life of Christ and are tremendously earnest about the things that have always been close to His heart. These men are serious about leading people to "higher ground" through their preaching. It is not uncommon for such preachers to spend long hours in preparation of their sermons and then still longer hours in preparation of their own souls and in agony before God over the souls of their congregation. When soul-to-soul preaching is done, ordinary results for this type of preaching may be anticipated. Hearers will feel the claims of Christ upon their lives. Conversions will occur. Personal holiness will be advanced. The angels of heaven will have reason to rejoice and the divine Saviour will be honored. The soul-to-soul preacher may hear people say, "Pastor, I need help. I realized today how lost I am!" or "Christ really spoke to me this morning and I have yielded to His Lordship." The results of such preaching could be described as extraordinary only if there were none—if no convictions were felt, if no changes occurred, if no spiritual advances were made.

I reaffirm that ordinary preaching produces ordinary results. Those who purpose to sound good when they preach may anticipate compliments. Those who seek to impart knowledge may expect to succeed. Those who yearn to see transformed lives and preach the Word of God in the power of the Holy Spirit will be prepared to see conversions and growth in personal holiness among their hearers.

However, revival is not the ordinary result of ordinary work. Revival is always extraordinary!

God has given gifts to men according to His own will and purpose. Men who exercise their gifts—whatever those gifts may be—will honor Christ and advance His cause. Ordinary gifts, exercised by ordinary men, produce ordinary results. The whole body of Christ relies upon these ordinary results. By these ordinary results the Church moves forward from generation to generation.

Occasionally, however, God Himself has taken ordinary men and through their ordinary efforts He has moved in an extraordinary fashion to produce truly extraordinary results. Pentecost was one of these occasions. Those who gathered in the Upper Room were people like us. They prayed as we pray. They waited on God as many of today's Christians have waited on God. But, God met them in a marvelous fashion, changing their feeble efforts into a mighty movement which turned the world upside down. The marvel of Pentecost is not the extraordinary nature of the men or their methods but the Holy Spirit and the results He produced.

The great sixteenth-century Reformation is another of those

extraordinary seasons. There is no human way to account for the splendid success of the Gospel under the preaching of such men as Luther, Calvin, Knox and a host of others, except to acknowledge that they labored in mighty days of revival.

America has seen revival also. The powerful effects of the preaching of George Whitefield, Jonathan Edwards, the Tennents, and a body of like-minded Christians can only be adequately described as the extraordinary movement of the Holy Spirit in revival.

Such was the case in 1857 when Jeremiah Lanphier, a simple man of faith and prayer, gathered a few businessmen for a noontime prayer meeting at the Old Dutch Church on Fulton Street in New York City. A handful of supplicants became a vast army of prayer warriors. A single prayer meeting turned into a nationwide prayer wave. Tens of thousands were converted, churches were transformed, society was benefited and the kingdom of God moved forward at a splendid rate. Why? Because great men were involved? Because new methods were utilized? No! No, indeed! It was God's doing. By an extraordinary move of His Holy Spirit, He created an extraordinary movement which produced extraordinary results.

If we persist in describing human efforts as revival and continue to think in terms of "annual revival meetings," believing that the work we are doing for God is revival, then we must content ourselves with far less than God is willing and able to give. If, on the other hand, we can realize that revival is truly God at work in a most unusual fashion, then our entire being can be stirred with longings and supplications to see just such an outpouring of God's mighty power in our own day.

The term *revive* suggests a return to consciousness or life. That which is revived becomes active or flourishing again. If consciousness and life are fully present—if everything is flourishing—revival is not needed and cannot be expected. Revival should be looked for during times of spiritual declension, during seasons of moral and spiritual bankruptcy and at those periods in the history of the Church when a "form of godliness" is present but the "power thereof" is denied.

Despite the tremendous amount of activity found in religious circles today, there is a very real sense in which the Church itself is like a sleeping giant. All the good that the Church is accomplishing throughout the world is nothing in comparison with the good that needs to be accomplished. The flurry of activity, so typical of evangelicalism, has still to awaken the sleeping giant. An increase in human endeavor may produce good fruit, but the great need is to revive that giant. Only God can accomplish this. When revival comes, the giant will not only stir and awaken, but also move with dynamic power and glorious impact.

Can you imagine the entire Body of Christ moving throughout the earth with unified purpose and Holy Spirit power? If that concept is too vast for your mind, think in terms of your own community. Consider every church in your community with every church member marching together in perfect harmony—every individual sharing precisely with every other individual the heartbeat of Jesus Christ. Imagine not one sleeping Christian left, not one backslidden believer remaining, but all alike devout and intent on seeing the will of Jesus Christ accomplished. To this startling picture add the same power of the Holy Spirit that transformed bumbling Peter into a Pentecost preacher. Unleash all this transforming power against the forces of sin and evil in your community. That is what revival is like.

THREE CHARACTERISTICS OF REVIVAL

In my description of revival as an extraordinary movement of the Holy Spirit producing extraordinary results, there are three specific issues that invite our consideration.

First, Revival Is Extraordinary

How long has it been since the world has experienced a general spiritual awakening? The majority of persons living in the western world would have to admit they have never seen revival. America has not known a large-scale general revival for more than 100 years. Revivals have become so scarce that much of the Church is hardly aware of their absence. When an entire generation of Christians can live and die without ever having come close to genuine revival, such a movement of God is extraordinary indeed!

Revivals must also be regarded as extraordinary because of the way they usually make their appearance in the world. There is a sense in which revival is like a prairie fire ignited by a bolt of lightning from the heavens. Without organization, advertising, or even sometimes human leadership, revivals have altered the hearts of men, the social attitudes of millions and the destinies of nations. On these precious occasions God Himself has stepped into the stream of history and done a work so mighty and wonderful that thereafter the mere retelling of God's acts is sufficient to excite expectation and longing in the hearts of the faithful.

True revival cannot be confined by state line, national boundaries, economic class systems, facial characteristics, skin coloring, educational distinctions, social status, or denominational preferences. Wherever God is, true revival can occur. When God speaks, the whole earth can hear. Revival can do as much for the suburbs as for the ghetto. The inner-city church can be as wonderfully transformed by revival as the church on the village green. Revival can penetrate the Iron Curtains of the world as readily as it can the Bamboo. The Spirit of God cannot be prevented from working where He wills. He can take an entire university and break it and remake it according to His own plan. Revival can as readily alter an entire nation as it can a local church. No human efforts or organized spiritual activity has such capacity. Revival can do what nothing else can and therefore must be described as truly extraordinary.

In the light of the extraordinary nature of revival, ought not Christians everywhere join the Psalmist in his prayer, "Wilt Thou not revive us again: that Thy people may rejoice in Thee?" (Psalm 85:6). Our concern for years has been with what we could do for God when instead we should have been pleading for Him to show what He could do for us. Surely in this we have great reason for shame and regret.

Second, Revival Is the Work of God

No amount of human effort can produce true revival. There is much that people can do. All that we can do we should do with all our might. Men can and must evangelize; it is part of the Great Commission. Men can and must train Christian workers if we are to honor our Lord's command. We can teach new converts the way of Christ and baptize them in the name of the Father, Son, and Holy Spirit. This, too, is part of the Great Commission. We can pray; this burden is placed upon every believer. We must concern ourselves with the social needs of the world to be true to the call of God to His church. Everything God has told us to do we ought to do, but having done it all, we must still wait upon Him to do what He alone can do. Revival comes from God. The sovereign Lord of the universe must revive us again or we will never know what true revival is. If God does not act, our churches will remain forever unrevived.

To whatever extent we fail to see God as the reviver of His people, to that extent we will fail to cry to Him day and night for this needed blessing. When Christians are fully persuaded that the God of all mercies is the God of revival and refuse to let God go until He blesses, then they may take hope that the heavens will soon be opened and God Himself will pour out such blessings that the whole world will scarcely be able to contain them.

Third, Revival Produces Extraordinary Results

A. Revival Includes A Tremendous Breaking

There are millions of people in the world today who profess to be "born-again," and while in many instances they can tell you the day and the hour in which they made their decision to accept Christ, all the evidence suggests they are suffering from a mighty delusion. Some professing Christians have lived in sin for years. There are religious workers whose greatest concern at all times has been their own comfort and security. Many regular church attenders consistently focus their minds on sporting events, business affairs or matters of personal interest as soon as the sermon begins. Many so-called worshipers can tell you what dress the pastor's wife wore in the service, but cannot recall the text of the sermon or the application of the message to their lives.

When revival comes, an intense spirit of conviction will be felt immediately. Conduct that has always seemed acceptable will appear unbelievably wicked. Prejudices that have characterized professing Christians for decades will be revealed for the grievous sins they really are. Private indulgences upon which a person has looked with favor for years will suddenly seem to merit all the wrath of God poured out forever. Prayerlessness, ignorance of Scripture, sins of omission and failure in good works will no longer be defended by a myriad of excuses, but will be laid open before "the God with whom we have to do."

Pride and self-centered living will no longer be excused as necessary defenses in a wicked world, but will be recognized as the very essence of wickedness itself. Words carelessly spoken will rise from their forgotten graves to haunt and torment until such a wave of conviction is felt that it will seem impossible to stand before it. Long forgotten sins against the members of the Body of Christ will be remembered with great grief. Indeed, when the revival comes, so powerful will be the conviction that persons who once thought themselves well worthy of heaven will stand in wonder and amazement that they are not already burning in the fires of hell.

When the revival comes, the agony over sin will be so great that the thought of prolonging life in the midst of such wickedness will be intolerable. From the very depths of men's beings will come the cry, "O God, save me from myself and sin, from my wickedness and depravity, or slay me; but do not let me persist another day in this awful condition."

The cross of Jesus Christ, which at one time might have seemed something of an enigma or a mystery, will now appear truly precious. It will be no longer possible for the convicted individual to think in terms of the death of Christ as generally needed for the sins of the world. So real will be his own sins that the cross will become of utmost importance to him. Having once been content to wear the cross as an ornament, the awakened will now view the horror of Christ's sufferings and realize that his very own sins put Christ there. In fact, the cross will become so personal that the wounds, bruises and stripes Jesus received, along with the insults, jeers and mental anguish, will provoke shame and sorrow that the innocent Saviour should have had to suffer so much for such an unworthy sinner.

These stirrings in the soul will drive the revived to a level of interest in the cross never before thought possible. All the devils in hell and all the servants of wickedness on earth will not have the power to keep the awakened sinner from consecration and devoted love to such a Saviour.

Long-standing habits of self-indulgence, subordinate neither to reason nor to God, will be broken when revival comes. The doors and walls of the prisons of self in which professing Christians have long been incarcerated will be broken down by revival. The Lord who came to declare freedom to the captives will make them free indeed. Sins that have been covered for decades will be brought to light and the fear of exposure and shame so long dreaded will now be thought nothing in comparison with the prospect of cleansing and renewal.

When revival comes, men may expect to have their well-laid plans broken. Schedules will be thrown to the wind. Goals and ambitions once thought to have the stamp of eternity upon them will now be revealed as temporal. Men who have lived in fear of others will be enabled to break with the past and to serve the living God as they have never served Him before. God's timing, God's purpose, God's plans, will rule the day. All that stands in resistance before Him may be expected to be broken and cast aside.

The breaking will affect not only individuals but also entire churches. Some churches may collapse when revival comes. Others which have been small and seemingly insignificant for years may suddenly be bursting their seams. Well-rehearsed choir numbers may remain unsung forever. Leaders of longstanding may find themselves forced into a corner of the church to watch and pray rather than to direct and lead. Traditions may perish. Programs may have to be abandoned. The status quo of the average church may come crashing to earth that God's own standards of holiness may prevail.

Pastors will be broken by revival. Men who have led large congregations may discover their ministry has the value of rubble. Sermons which seemed satisfactory enough in previous days will never do for revival. Habits and practices acceptable in a sleeping church will either be broken when revival comes or the pastor himself may lose his ministry. A *revived people* must have a *revived minister.* Nothing else will do and nothing else should be offered.

B. Revival Includes A Remaking

God, the Master Workman, will not break all before Him in a mighty wave of destruction only to retire once more to His heaven. When God breaks He can also be counted upon to remake. When revival comes, people and pastors and churches will be gloriously remade.

Broken men are pliant men. When a person has reached the end of himself, he is ready for a new beginning. The broken individual has no inclination or ability to tell God how to proceed. He is ready for any changes God desires and is now able to regard whatever God does as a source of perpetual thanksgiving.

When God remakes people, He shapes them with a new center— God Himself becomes that center. What God wants is now the only thing that matters. Prior to being revived, the individual may have desired to do God's will but also desired to do his own will. He allowed the will of God to be crowded out and his own will prevailed. But now he finds God's will central in his thinking and desire. Even more glorious, he now finds himself enabled to do God's will, for the very God that revived him is an enabling God. Thus, a life which had been earlier marked by self-seeking, love of money, delight in ease and pleasure and careless attitudes toward spiritual things is now marked by an earnest and consistent desire to please God.

The newly revived remembers sins long ago forgotten and now is unable and unwilling to conceal those sins any longer. As the light of God's truth shines upon him he knows what he must do. He begins apologizing for lies, paying long overdue debts and making restitution whenever and wherever needed.

Confession of sin becomes the order of the day. Those who have sinned in private will make their confession before God, whom they have wronged. Individuals who have sinned against other individuals will go to those persons and make their peace. Those who have sinned publicly will find the grace of Christ to make public confessions. A watching world will stand in astonishment as Christians who have lived like heathen now begin to manifest the love of Christ for one another and as biblical commandments and principles long trampled in the dust are suddenly revered and restored to practice.

Revived individuals are also marked by their great interest in the Word of God. Most professing Christians are content to let their pastors or Bible teachers do the digging for them in the Word of God, but revived individuals find themselves desiring the "sincere milk of the Word as newborn babes." They soon learn to relish the strong meat of the Word and to delight in lengthy, deep, reverent, practical and searching teaching and preaching. Even more, they will be moved to diligent study of the Bible and to faithful application of its wonderful truths to their lives.

Prayer, which may have seemed drudgery prior to the revival, will become pure delight. The "sweet hour of prayer," instead of being merely the words of a song, will become a precious reality. Rather than inventing a host of excuses for not praying, the revived finds no other activity so delightful or beneficial. When the allotted time for prayer is up, instead of gratitude that the chore is over, there will be sorrow that the time has passed so swiftly. And why is this so? Simply because the revived Christian has fallen in love. The prime desire of every lover is to be with his beloved. So it is in revival.

Agony for souls will also characterize the revived. Perfunctory witnessing will no longer do. Shallow decisions on the part of others will not be acceptable. Nothing short of true and lasting conversions will satisfy. Prayer for the eternal welfare of others will become a passion. A deep and searching ministry of the Holy Spirit must be had. The same liberating Spirit that broke and remade them is what they yearn for in their family, among their friends and throughout the world.

Holiness will become a prime object of life. "To be like Jesus" will become the theme song of the revived. "Oh, to be like Him" will be the desire governing their thought and conduct. The great principles of Holy Scripture will no longer be relegated to discussion on Sunday but lived on a daily basis. The mighty Word of God will act as the very sword of the Spirit to put to flight Satan, the enemy of the soul.

C. Revival Includes A Pouring-forth

Fervor and excitement characterize the revived. The dull, apathetic attitude, common in much of Christendom, will no longer prevail. With the very life of God surging in the soul, the revived will be gripped by intense earnestness and a spirit of expectation. The God that raised up Jesus from the dead has raised them from their own graves of sin. The power that lifted the exalted Saviour to the heavens and placed Him on the right hand of the Father is working in them with quickening might. The same Saviour who was made Lord over all is now their Lord. In the grace of that Saviour's Spirit and with the fervor stirred by the knowledge of that Saviour's glory, these revived Christians are ready to take on a world of sin and darkness. Believing that God Himself will also intercede on behalf of others as He has on their behalf, they will march out of the revival circle as a conquering army. Thus, the very revival that broke and then remade men and women will pour forth upon an unsuspecting world with the same breaking and remaking power.

A revived people become the instruments of revival. The remade become the instruments of remaking. The recipients of grace become the instruments of grace dispensed. Those who confessed their sins now hear the confessions of others. Those who were in need of prayer are now teaching men to pray. Those who could never stand firm in holiness for a single day are now pillars of holiness raised by God for all the world to see.

Now new converts will be made without arm twisting. Now elaborate plans to follow-up are not needed, for God the Holy Spirit is at work. Now instead of pleading and cajoling with men to take a stand for Christ, the earnest presentation of the basic doctrines of the Bible will carry the revival forward in ever increasing force. Wave upon wave of divine blessing will break upon the parched earth, for God Himself has worked, and all the praise and glory are due His name.

The social concerns, so long languishing in the hands of infirm and uncaring Christians, will take on new meaning in the light of revival. What men could not be made to do by any human effort is now accomplished with ease by divine enabling. Men who never had a serious thought for the welfare of anyone outside their own immediate circle will earnestly desire to see all men treated kindly. Great causes that have suffered for lack of funding will find revived men and women willing to give and ready to help. What no person could do by himself and what no group effort of men could accomplish, the Lord God Almighty will accomplish in the wake of mighty revival.

The most wonderful aspect of the breaking and the remaking and the pouring forth of true revival is that God does it all. If men could produce revival, they would stand back and glory in their handiwork. But when God who is dependent upon no man or church does it, every single revived individual will have cause to praise Him without ceasing. Here is the very reason the Psalmist prays, "Wilt thou not revive us again: that Thy people may rejoice in Thee?"

Revival is indeed an extraordinary movement of the Holy Spirit producing extraordinary results. May the God of revival deliver us from contentment with the ordinary while He stands ready to do the extraordinary.

Chapter Two

When

Is

Revival

Needed?

Wherever there are proofs of spiritual death in or around the professing church—wherever there is an actual decay or dormancy in the energy or activity of its members, or whenever there is the absence of a progression in those habits and feelings and principles that distinguish the divine life, there is a necessity for a revival. If among the professors of a holy faith, we find a growing conformity to the world in its passions, its policy, or its practices, a want of sensibility to the claims of God, to the glory of Jesus, or to the imperishable interests of immortal souls, a deadness in devotion, a lack of spirituality in sentiment and feeling, a willingness to parade a dwarfed and shrivelled Christianity before the world as if it were the healthful and full grown impersonation of a living and energetic faith—we say a revival is necessary; and this notwithstanding any scattered and splendid exceptions of almost Apostolic zeal or seraphic fervor, that may give lustre or dignity to the age of the church with which they are connected.

John MacNaughtan, Paisley, Scotland

When Is Revival Needed?

When the Word of the Lord came to Jeremiah confirming his ordination as a prophet to the nations, he hesitated modestly, saying, *Ah, Lord God! behold I cannot speak: for I am a child.* But the Lord who calls also equips. He told Jeremiah in no uncertain terms, *Say not, I am a child: for thou shalt go to all that I shall send thee, and whatsoever I command thee thou shalt speak. Be not afraid of their faces: for I am with thee to deliver thee, saith the Lord* (Jeremiah 1:6-8).

Just as the time approached for Jeremiah to begin his public ministry, the Lord said,

> *Thou therefore gird up thy loins, and arise, and speak unto them all that I command thee: be not dismayed at their faces, lest I confound thee before them. For, behold, I have made thee this day a defenced city, and an iron pillar, and brasen walls against the whole land, against the kings of Judah, against the princes thereof, against the priests thereof, and against the people of the land. And they shall fight against thee; but they shall not prevail against thee; for I am with thee, saith the Lord, to deliver thee* (Jeremiah 1:17-19).

He was one man against an entire nation!

He was one man with an unwanted message!

He was one man with the God-given courage to use a much-despised term!

Jeremiah plastered Israel with a label they did not like and could not peel off! Jeremiah laid his axe to the root of Israel's tree and in specific, direct, and plain-spoken fashion fixed attention on Israel's great problem! Fearing neither princes, priests, prophets nor people, he denounced them all alike!

He called their problem *backsliding.* For his faithful declaration of the truth of God, he received as much thanks and acclaim as he would if he were to declare the same message in the churches today.

Ponder this searching passage:

> *Why then is this people of Jerusalem slidden back by a perpetual backsliding? They hold fast deceit, they refuse to return. I hearkened and heard, but they spake not aright: no man repented him of his wickedness, saying, What have I done?*

Every one turned to his course, as the horse rusheth into the battle. Yea, the stork in the heaven knoweth her appointed times; and the turtle [dove] and the crane and the swallow observe the time of their coming; but my people know not the judgment of the Lord (Jeremiah 8:5-7).

How is it that the so-called *brute beasts* and *dumb birds* are wiser than men? The salmon know when and where to return to their place of beginnings, but the backslider has forgotten the God who made him. *The ox knoweth his owner, and the ass his master's crib,* cried Isaiah, *but Israel doth not know, my people doth not consider. Ah sinful nation, a people laden with iniquity, a seed of evildoers, children that are corrupters: they have forsaken the LORD, they have provoked the Holy One of Israel unto anger, they are gone away backward* (Isaiah 1:3,4).

What exactly is backsliding? Nowhere in all Scripture is it better described than in Proverbs 14:14a: *The backslider in heart shall be filled with his own ways.* There you have it—a backslider is a person who was once emptied of his own ways and filled with the ways of God, but gradually allowed his own ways to seep back in until he is all but empty of God and full of himself again.

This is the exact problem Jeremiah addresses. The people of his day had allowed more and more of self to crowd into their hearts until the God who had brought them out of Egypt and blessed them above all human beings was almost entirely crowded out of their lives and forgotten. Chapters two and three of Jeremiah clearly outline this crowding-out process. The word from God to backslidden Israel commences with a lament concerning the former days: *I remember thee, the kindness of thy youth, the love of thine espousals, when thou wentest after me in the wilderness, in a land that was not sown. Israel was holiness unto the LORD, and the firstfruits of His increase...* (2:2b,3). What was had ceased to be. Their early love for God was gone. Holiness had become a forgotten term. Israel no longer delighted the heart of God. A people who had once borne fruit were barren. Men and women formerly filled with God were now filled with themselves. Consider carefully the unfolding evidence:

1. *Thus saith the LORD, What iniquity have your fathers found in me, that they are gone far from me, and have walked after vanity, and are become vain?* (2:5). In the vanity of their own minds and hearts, they had determined God was not as important to them as He had formerly been. Thus, they crowded Him out.

2. They conveniently forgot the great things God had done for them in former days: bringing them out of the land of Egypt, leading them through the wilderness, and bringing them into a plentiful country (2:6,7). Whenever the great mercies of God are forgotten,

praise and thanksgiving are easily crowded out.

3. Even the religious leaders of Israel had joined the backsliding hosts. The priests failed to ask, *Where is the LORD?* Those responsible for handling the law did not know God. The pastors also transgressed against the Lord, and the prophets joined the forces of Baal (2:8). Thus, all the religious leaders engaged in activities totally devoid of spiritual benefit. In so doing, they crowded the God of Israel out of their religious functions.

4. With the God of Israel crowded out of their lives, they were free to cast about for something else to take His place. Not being altogether godless in their thinking, they foolishly adopted as gods mere figments of the imaginations of men—gods that were no gods— a truly astonishing and horrible departure from the glory the people had once known and enjoyed. Jeremiah wonders if any other nation ever exchanged its gods, especially *the God,* for no gods (2:11,12).

5. Israel had once drunk at the fountain of living waters, but having now crowded God out of their lives, they had begun to hew out for themselves broken cisterns that could hold no water (2:13). Imagine, the living waters of a fountain exchanged for the stagnant water of a cistern—and a leaking cistern at that.

6. People who had once known the guiding and correcting power of a holy fear of God, so absolutely essential to life and happiness, had crowded this anchor right out of their lives and had begun drifting on the vast seas of the backslidden (2:19).

7. Despite continual disclaimers of any pollution and repeated washings with nitre and soap, the filth of their backslidden condition was upon them. It could not be scrubbed off. Having played the harlot under every green tree, they could not hide their iniquity (2:22,23).

8. What could be more natural than for men and women who have crowded the living God right out of their lives to worship and serve the things they have made with their own hands rather than the Creator who made them? (2:27,28). In a time of trouble they might call to a stick and say, *Thou art my father,* or to a stone and say, *Thou hast brought me forth.* But can such gods save? Never!

9. As with backsliders of all times and places, once they had completely crowded God and holiness out of their lives, they could not be content until they had drawn others into their circle of corruption (2:33,34). A great delight of the fallen is the fall of others, but the blood of their victims is upon their *skirts* (v.34).

10. Despite these overwhelming evidences of backsliding in Israel, Judah did not return to the Lord with all her heart but only deceptively so that faithless Israel was less treacherous than Judah (3:10, 11).

When God sent Jeremiah to proclaim this message, He did not

lead him to believe that Israel was expectantly waiting for a prophet to come and reclaim them. Jeremiah was clearly told, *They shall fight against thee.* And they did. Backsliders are notorious fighters. Returning from their backsliding requires tremendous grace. Note this demand, *Return, thou backsliding Israel, saith the LORD; and I will not cause mine anger to fall upon you: for I am merciful, saith the LORD, and I will not keep anger forever. Only acknowledge thine iniquity, that thou hast transgressed against the LORD thy God, and hast scattered thy ways to the strangers under every green tree, and ye have not obeyed My voice, saith the LORD. Turn, O backsliding children...* (3:12-14).

When God sent Jeremiah, it was with a message not merely for the common people but for the kings and princes and priests as well. Imagine the anger kindled among religious leaders when God used Jeremiah's tongue to declare *I will give you pastors according to mine heart, which shall feed you with knowledge and understanding* (3:15). If it takes grace for people to repent of their backsliding, how much more grace is required for backslidden pastors to repent not only of their own sins but also of the evil of misleading their people? Imagine the fight Jeremiah faced with those backslidden leaders whom God promised to replace!

When God sent Jeremiah, however, it was not only with the promise of a coming fight, but also with the promise of certain victory: *They shall not prevail against thee; for I am with thee, saith the LORD, to deliver thee* (1:19). Every backslider must face this fact—he is engaged in a fight he is certain to lose. Backsliders never prevail against the God they have crowded out of their lives.

While the term *backsliding* is not used constantly throughout the Bible, the problem of backsliding itself is evident everywhere. Beginning with Genesis 6:5,6 where we are told, ...*GOD saw that the wickedness of man was great in the earth, and that every imagination of the thoughts of his heart was only evil continually. And it repented the LORD that He had made man on the earth, and it grieved Him at His heart,* and continuing to the Revelation of John where Jesus Himself said, *Nevertheless I have somewhat against thee, because thou hast left thy first love* (2:4), man's capacity to grieve his Creator by being filled with himself is abundantly evident.

The problem of backsliding is not a phenomenon peculiar to one age or people. The temptation to backslide is constant with the people of God. The sin of backsliding, however, is not always prevalent to the same degree. It was definitely a great evil in the days of Moses. Hosea felt deeply the burden of the same evil as did Isaiah and other prophets. In New Testament days the Jews manifested tragic backsliding. Now, in our own day, this great evil is prevalent once more. Literally millions of professing Christians show serious signs of severe backsliding.

God is infinitely patient and understanding of the weaknesses of His people, but backsliding is not merely a problem of human weakness. Backsliding is the sin of crowding God out by filling one's life with self. Many of us who are astonished and disgusted that a dog will return to his vomit still fail to consider carefully Peter's warning,

> For it had been better for them not to have known the way of righteousness, than, after they have known it, to turn from the holy commandment delivered unto them. But it is happened unto them according to the true proverb, the dog is turned to his own vomit again; and the sow that was washed to her wallowing in the mire (Second Peter 2:21,22).

Here is a very accurate description of backsliding: the washed pig wallowing once more in the mire and the dog eagerly lapping up his own vomit!

What more powerfully proclaims the need of revival in our day than the backslidden condition of hosts of professing Christians? The people of Jeremiah's day had no edge on us in this terrible departure from the living God. If there ever were a people wallowing in mud like pigs and consuming their own vomit like dogs, it is the people of our own day. We delight in our vast progress and entertain ourselves with stories of the wonderful increase of knowledge in our lifetime, but the love of that which is filthy and vile has scarcely ever been greater in the history of the world. We pride ourselves in our understanding and in our love of the downtrodden and oppressed; we do not hesitate to advise the rest of the world on how to conduct its affairs; but we are so deeply embedded in the quagmire of self that all our mouthings are nothing but dirty bubbles.

EVIDENCES OF A BACKSLIDDEN CONDITION

Backslidden Christians are evident everywhere. They are in the churches and out of the churches. They are in the pews and in the pulpits. They are on boards and are bored. They serve on committees and teach Sunday school. The backslidden seem to be more numerous than the upright and their influence throughout the world vastly more profound. While backsliders do not all manifest the same traits, evidences of their condition are not difficult to pinpoint. The following characteristics merit our serious attention.

1. **When prayer ceases to be a vital part of a professing Christian's life, backsliding is present.** It is shocking to realize that many churches have no public prayer meetings of any kind. More upsetting is the fact that many individual Christians have no regular stated seasons of private prayer during which they commune alone with

God. How can a person be both Christian and prayerless? However, prayer does not need to be entirely lacking from a person's life for backsliding to prevail. When prayer becomes perfunctory and without moral earnestness, there is more than ample evidence of backsliding. Some who *say* their prayers every day never pray. The formulation of thoughts and ideas along religious lines, the mouthing of words, the bowing of the head and body and the repetition of phrases, do not in and of themselves constitute real prayer. If the heart does not earnestly commune with God, no genuine prayer is present. The mere repetition of written prayers, no matter how beautifully constructed or seemingly sincere, does not guarantee genuine prayer. When the heart of man and the heart of God meet in communion, there is prayer. Prayerlessness and mere formality in saying prayers are unmistakable marks of a backslidden condition.

2. When the quest for biblical truth ceases and one grows content with the knowledge of eternal things already acquired, there can be no mistaking the presence of backsliding. Almost all backsliders demonstrate a sense of satisfaction with the truth already in their possession. Backsliders are rarely diligent in their study of the Bible. They do not find themselves in the grip of a passion to mine treasures from the Word of God. They are content with the little pearls of wisdom their mothers hung about their necks in the days of their spiritual infancy or with the gems the pastor mines on their behalf. They do not find themselves daily in the garden of the Lord plucking flowers rare and fragrant. They are content with the wilted bouquet they carried to their baptism. If any new biblical truth comes to them, it must come by the effort of another, not their own. This is not to say backsliders never read the Bible. Many backsliders have long established habits of dutiful devotion they have never broken, but while they go on reading Bible words, backsliders are content with the truth of God in their possession.

3. When the biblical knowledge possessed or acquired is treated as external fact and not applied inwardly, backsliding is present. Not every backslider has totally abandoned the acquisition of biblical truth. Some badly backslidden pastors acquire new Bible knowledge on a weekly basis. It is possible to go on learning new things from the Holy Scriptures without benefit to the soul. If biblical truth does not enter the heart and transform the life, its acquisition is without eternal merit. The Bible was designed by God not merely to inform us, but to transform us. If biblical truth already possessed is not acted upon, the accumulation of additional truth will have little or no effect. Some backsliders teach Sunday school every week. They carefully prepare their lessons and diligently consider the facts they are to present. However, if their contemplation and their teaching of the Word of God do not move from the area of the head to the realm of the heart, no amount of additional study and teaching will alter their backslidden ways. Likewise, the backslider may sit in a Bible-preaching church every time the doors are open. He may listen attentively to the words spoken and congratulate the preacher on his unfolding of biblical truth, but if that Word does not drive out self, his backslidden condition only worsens every time he hears the Bible proclaimed.

4. **When earnest thoughts about eternal things cease to be regular and gripping, it should be like a warning light to the backslider.** In the early days of a person's new walk with Christ, the mind continually turns toward spiritual matters. When backsliding commences, the mind turns less and less toward heaven, God, eternity and holiness. In the earliest stages of the decline, spiritual thoughts may come frequently, but they are less gripping. As a person becomes more and more filled with his own ways, there will simply be less room for thoughts of eternity. At first, there may be a conscious awareness that the thought patterns are changing, but as backsliding progresses, it becomes less and less obvious to the backslider that this transformation is taking place. Eventually, a gentle rebuke will be treated with scorn and the backslider will rise to justify his own departure from the living God.

5. **When the services of the church lose their delights, a backslidden condition probably exists.** The recently converted find participation in the services of the church a thrill and a joy. They never think they will grow weary of these newly discovered blessings. The singing of every hymn is an experience to be remembered. The hearing of the Scriptures read publicly is sheer delight. They sit on the edges of their seats to hear the sermon and can scarcely find sufficient words to thank the preacher for his immense contribution to their lives. Not content to come only on Sunday mornings, they may even shock the elders by their presence at every stated meeting of the church. Then backsliding sets in. "What happened to the preacher?" they wonder. "How did he lose his fire? Why do the once stirring hymns now seem to drag?" Even the Scriptures lose their cutting edge. The backslider now finds it difficult to attend even the Sunday morning service. The warmhearted approach of the pastor and the people now seem meddlesome. Rather than risk an uncomfortable conversation with an overzealous deacon, the backslider slips out quickly from the service and makes his way home, spiritually hungry and unsatisfied. Finding no help in such a church, he either abandons attendance altogether or seeks a church home where backsliders are more comfortable.

6. **When pointed spiritual discussions are an embarrassment, that is certain evidence of backsliding.** The person on fire for Jesus Christ delights in every opportunity to talk about Him. No place

seems inappropriate for vital spiritual conversation. When backsliding begins, the church seems like the best place to discuss religious matters. Soon it seems altogether inappropriate to speak seriously of spiritual matters in mixed company. It isn't long before free discussion of eternal matters becomes a source of acute embarrassment. If anyone takes the liberty of addressing the backslider concerning the welfare of his soul on a street corner, in an airplane or on a commuter train, his temper may flare. For fear of public confrontation, the backslider is apt to make fun of a serious-minded co-worker who persists in speaking freely of spiritual issues on the job. The backslider is apt to go so far as to proclaim vehemently, "There are two things I never discuss— religion and politics." Mark this, if the public discussion of deeply important spiritual matters is an embarrassment to you, there can be no question concerning your backslidden condition. The person whose love for Christ is current will delight in every opportunity, public or private, to hear Him lifted up with reverence.

7. **When sports, recreation and entertainment are a large and necessary part of your lifestyle, you may assume backsliding is in force.** Paul acknowledged there was profit in physical exercise. Jesus demonstrated the worth of drawing aside from daily tasks for rest and revitalization. However, the current focus on games and entertainment has nothing in common with a biblical lifestyle. So serious has become man's love of entertainment that some churches even compete with one another for a star-studded cast to lead their public services. Few churches even consider holding special meetings in competition with sporting events. Many a preacher is more certain to have the Sunday morning service over by noon sharp than he is to say anything worthwhile. He would no sooner incur the wrath of his recreation-minded congregation by detaining them from Sunday afternoon picnics and games than he would deprive himself of his own Saturday evening entertainment.

Christians are not saved to play but to serve. If sporting events are as important to you as spiritual progress, you are backslidden. If you must choose between church and recreation and recreation wins, you are backslidden. If you devote more time to play and exercise than to prayer and the Word of God, there can be no doubt of your true spiritual condition. In your case, backsliding has not only begun, but progressed to a deplorable level.

8. **When sins of the body and of the mind can be indulged in without an uproar in your conscience, your backslidden condition is certain.** Prior to conversion it is to be expected that sins will play havoc with the conscience. The unregenerate is known to have a seared conscience and can hardly be required to shed tears over sins. But how can a Christian, who has been made a new creature in

Christ Jesus, for whom *all things have become new,* manifest this same callousness? By one method only: backsliding.

When a Christian is walking in fellowship with Jesus Christ, he has a sensitivity to right and wrong similar to that which characterized Jesus in His life on earth. But let that walk with Christ deteriorate and sensitivity will vanish. The backslider is characterized by his disregard for personal sin. What once seemed almost inconceivably awful becomes too insignificant to worry about. Sins that were once carefully shunned the backslider now embraces with relish. As the backslider grows more and more full of himself, he looks with increasing warmth upon those sins of body and mind which will make his position comfortable and pleasant, demonstrate his freedom from unnecessary restraints and prove that he is as able to discern good from evil as the Almighty. Once sick at the mere thought of sin, the backslider can now engage in gross iniquity with scarcely a stir of conscience or a tear of grief.

9. When aspirations for Christlike holiness cease to be dominant in your life and thinking, backsliding is there. For the backslidden, holiness seems both unattainable and unnecessary. Not so for the earnest Christian who takes to heart the biblical injunction *...Be ye holy: for I am holy* (First Peter 1:16). Knowing the truth of the words, *holiness, without which no man shall see the Lord* (Hebrews 12:14), the active Christian makes biblical holiness the great goal of his life. Every time he falls short, even by a fraction, he is grieved and confesses his shortcomings to the Lord with pleas for help that he might do better.

Not so the backslider. Weary of the claims of God upon his life, he crowds out aspirations to holiness with self-centeredness until thoughts of holiness lose their grip and actually become somewhat repugnant to him. Whereas he once lived to be holy, he would now sooner die than be holy. Having choked out the love of holiness, the backslider finds contentment in his current condition. He neither hungers nor thirsts for righteousness nor feels grief for its lack.

10. When the acquisition of money and goods becomes a dominant part of your thinking, you have clear confirmation of backsliding. When a professed Christian begins to focus on money, cars, houses, lands, stocks, bonds and adornments, he is clearly on the course of the backslider. The Bible does not condemn the possession of money or of goods, neither does it prohibit their broad use, but in no uncertain language it forbids the love of money and a heart attachment to things. The believer is expected to live as a pilgrim who is passing through this world of goods. He must not attach his heart to that which is perishing, but set his affection on *things above.* He must lay his treasures up in heaven where moth and rust cannot corrupt and where thieves cannot break through and steal.

The backslider will not live by these standards. He cannot bear to see so much wealth around him without laying up his own share. To live for eternity—so faraway indeed when the present is all around him—is a task in which the backslider will no longer engage. When you find yourself grasping after the here and now, take heed, your backsliding is showing.

11. When you can mouth religious songs and words without heart, be sure backsliding is present. Much public singing of hymns and Gospel music must be utterly distasteful to God. Consider the ease with which Christians sing,

My Jesus, I love Thee, I know Thou art mine,
For Thee all the follies of sin I resign

when no abandonment of sin is intended and no fresh love of Christ is present, or

Sweeter as the years go by...

when bitterness fills the heart more and more with each passing year.

Contemplate the often repeated prayer, *Thy will be done on earth, as it is in heaven,* lifted Sunday after Sunday by men and women who steadfastly refuse to do the will of God themselves and are surely in no position to assist its accomplishment in the lives of others. Consider testimony meetings in which only events of years ago are narrated because the speaker has no current experience with the Lord which he can share. The ability to mouth religious phrases, songs, prayers and testimonies without depth of feeling is a certain sign of backsliding. Every honest Christian can expect occasions when he bows to the will of God only with the greatest of difficulty, but on such occasions he has the grace of silence. The backslider, however, finds no difficulty speaking hypocritically. To mouth the words and phrases of affection and commitment actually foreign to his own heart poses no greater difficulty than continuing in his backslidden condition.

12. When you can hear the Lord's name taken in vain, spiritual concerns mocked and eternal issues flippantly treated, and not be moved to indignation and action, you are backslidden. The true Christian not only reverences God's name, but also cannot bear the misuse of God's name by others without deep hurt and sorrow. To remain silent among mockers is a restraint godly people cannot stomach. To hear sacred things treated with contempt and eternal matters treated lightly without indignation is beyond the ability of all who truly love God with all their hearts and minds. Those who walk in fellowship with Christ must be expected to take their stand against all such works of darkness.

The backslider has no trouble mingling with the profane. Their contemptuous and filthy language brings no grief to his soul. To offend the swearer by gently asking him to refrain from irreverent speech is unthinkable to the backslider. To leave the room because the tone of the conversation is degrading would never occur to the long-established backslider. That would require far more courage and love for God than the backslider knows.

13. **When you can watch degrading movies and television and read morally debilitating literature, you can be sure you have backslidden.** That movies, television, and literature are getting more degenerate with each passing year should be obvious. Imagine Christians allowing themselves to be contaminated by this filth of the world. Would Jesus go with you to the theatre to watch the movie of your choice? Would he join your family television circle and watch with you each hour? Could He sanction all that you read? If not, you have clear evidence of backsliding. Whenever a Christian does anything Jesus will not sanction, he is in deep trouble. If you cannot control what you watch and read, you would be better off without eyes. Did not Jesus say it would be better for a man to pluck out his own eyes rather than be led to lust by what he gazed upon? The Christian should take Jesus' words seriously and avoid temptation rather than be corrupted. The backslider will think of those who refuse to be corrupted by what they watch as narrow-minded bigots. The backslider will defend his right to read anything published and will read whatever pleases him, advertising his broad-mindedness in the process. No more evidence of backsliding than this is needed.

14. **When breaches of peace in the brotherhood are of no concern to you, that is proof of backsliding.** The unity of His Body is a matter of great concern to Jesus Christ. The entire prayer of John seventeen focuses on this topic. Many of the Apostolic letters plead for unity. Clear biblical guidelines have been laid down for the preservation of unity and its restoration when broken. Every individual with a heart in tune with God is deeply concerned about the unity of the Church. This unity cannot be broken without grief to the believer. The godly person will do nothing to break the unity, nor will he remain silent while others are destroying it.

Not so the backslider. What does the unity of the Church mean to him? The backslider finds no problem in splitting a church over insignificant issues. He feels no compunction over leading a church split. If no doctrinal issues are available over which to divide the "One Body," the backslider is content to divide it over personalities. The backslider feels no great grief when the fellowship of believers is broken any more than he feels joy when the fellowship is preserved in unity. Personal concerns are always greater in importance to the backslider than overwhelming Bible truth. Like the apostates Jude renounced, backsliders separate themselves for sensual reasons (v.19). While Jesus pronounced His blessing upon the peacemaker, the backslider is content to find his blessing elsewhere.

15. When the slightest excuse seems sufficient to keep you from spiritual duty and opportunity, you are backslidden. While the soul prospers, duty and opportunity are seized with joy. Faithful Christians delight in the very prospects of usefulness. But let spiritual backsliding begin and opportunities of service once regarded with enthusiasm become burdens too heavy to bear. The backslider becomes a master excuse-maker. Whereas earlier he would have laughed with astonishment at the feeble excuses of other backsliders, he is now able to offer the most unlikely reasons for his failure to take his spiritual responsibilities seriously. He even expects those who hear his excuses to believe his unworthy lies. He cannot attend prayer meeting in the evening "because...." and certainly not in the morning "because...." He cannot usher on Sunday "because...." You name it and he will have an excuse to explain why he cannot do it. It is not simply that the excuses are usually flimsy, often inconsistent with the real facts, seldom more than slightly accurate, and never appropriate for a professing Christian, but that the excuse-maker is hardly aware of the fallen condition his excuses represent. The backslider is often the last to know his real condition. By then it may be humanly impossible to reclaim him.

16. When you become content with your lack of spiritual power and no longer seek repeated enduements of power from on high, you have backslidden. The growing Christian, characterized by spiritual yearnings and restlessness, wants more and more of God's grace and fullness. Every experience in the Christian's pilgrimage is but a stimulus to new heights. Yesterday's growth is a reminder of tomorrow's needs and opportunities. A fresh outpouring of God's power and grace whets the appetite for yet another. A precious time in prayer and the Word is an encouragement to further times of prayer and Bible study. However, this is not true for the backslider who is content to sit back and enjoy what he has already experienced. Let others go on seeking power with God; he has found all he wants. Let others press on towards new goals; the backslider is comfortable where he is. No intimations of Spirit outpourings, no descriptions of lofty spiritual heights, and no appeals to fresh consecration disturb his slumbers.

17. When you pardon your own sin and sloth by saying the Lord understands and remembers that we are dust, you have revealed your backslidden condition. Of course, God understands! Certainly He remembers that we are dust, but what has God's understanding to do with our sin and sloth? Christians are not called to take their ease. Christians were not born of the Spirit of God in order that they might continue in sin. To continue in sin and to tolerate sloth on the pretext of appreciating the grace of God are presumptions of the worst sort. This evil approach is certainly not new. When the Apostle

Paul asked, *Shall we continue in sin, that grace may abound?* he vehemently answered his own question by declaring, *God forbid. How shall we that are dead to sin, live any longer therein?* (Romans 6:1,2). Willingness to condone or pardon one's own sin and spiritual sloth is a certain sign of backsliding.

18. When there is no music in your soul and no song in your heart, the silence testifies to your backsliding. The healthy Christian is characterized by a spirit of praise. Even those without musical talents will make *a joyful noise unto the Lord* when their souls are in health. The spirit of praise and thankfulness is always the spirit of the growing believer. Past mercies are strong in the memories of prosperous souls. Psalms of thanksgiving fill the hearts of those who walk with God. But let a little backsliding begin and praise turns to murmuring. Thousands of special mercies from the hands of God can be forgotten in the face of one small affliction. Mark the changing attitude of the Israelites who could not remember with thanks the mercies of their God. They fell from the place of sweet praise to backsliding, murmuring and complaining against God and their divinely appointed leaders. The song was snatched from their hearts. The joy was gone from their experience. Backsliding was their lot and portion. It is the same with backsliders of every generation.

Has the music gone from your soul? Are your songs of praise without the ring of joy? Have the past mercies of God grown dim? Do you even now chafe under the lightest hand of affliction? Do you find yourself in the grip of a complaining spirit? What further evidence of backsliding do you require?

19. When you adjust happily to the world's lifestyle, your own mirror will tell the truth of your backsliding. The world sees no great problem with unpaid debts. Bankruptcy is perfectly acceptable among today's godless businessmen. Dishonesty as a way of life is as acceptable in most business circles as profit. Lying is hardly noticed and certainly considered excusable as the means to a good end.

Can the Christian accept such behavior? No, he is required to renounce the hidden things of dishonesty, to resist walking in craftiness and to cease handling the truth deceitfully (Second Corinthians 4:2). With hearty earnestness the growing Christian conforms to biblical standards of righteousness; not so the backslider. Bills are carelessly or deliberately paid late or left unpaid. Backslidden Christians take bankruptcy as a way out of legal obligations without serious twinges of conscience. Lying is also common for the backslider. Backslidden Christians tell people what they want to hear just as the ungodly do. Appointments are not kept. Promises, even to pray for a need, are not remembered. Many commitments are never honored. When you find yourself able to fit into the world's way of debt, be sure you have backslidden. When your word is not binding and truth is not to be found in your inner self, the brand *backslider* is rightly yours.

20. When injustice and human misery exist around you and you do little or nothing to relieve the suffering, be sure you are backslidden. The Lord Jesus Christ was marked by compassion; so are all His followers. By disposition, some are more attentive to the needs of those around them than others, but every genuine Christian must be sensitive to the hurts of others and minister with the grace and mercy of Jesus as he is able. Unlike Christ, the backslider is content to inquire, *Who is my neighbor?* and pass to the other side of the road. Whenever you are willing to turn a need into an intellectual discussion, you have been marked by the backsliders's pen. Giving a cup of cold water in the Saviour's name is still an elementary requirement for faithful disciples of the Lord Jesus. If your eyes are blind to the sufferings of humanity on every hand and your heart is sealed by indifference, the testimony of your backslidden condition is so loud and eloquent the whole world can mark your condition.

21. When your church has fallen into spiritual declension and the Word of God is no longer preached there with power and you are still content, you are in a backslidden condition. It was never God's plan for any church to exist without divine power. More than a few churches are dead, however, and the spiritual power has been gone for so long that this condition has become the accepted norm. But should it be? Jesus Himself is never in decline or lacking in power. The believer has no reason to accept declension and powerlessness in his church, and if he does, he needs to face his own backslidden condition. It is not fair to blame the pastor. Surely he may be partially responsible, but take the condition of your church to heart. If you were always fervent in spirit, instant in season and out of season, ready in prayer and quick to lift and encourage in all that is right and holy, would your church be where it is now? Perhaps you cannot change the condition of your church, but you can surely help the condition of your own soul. If declension and powerlessness mark your church, they need not mark you. If you are content with those conditions in your church, it is proof of your own backslidden situation.

22. When the spiritual condition of the world declines around you and you cannot perceive it, that is testimony of your backslidden stance. Growing Christians are perceptive. Just as Jesus could discern signs of spiritual health and vitality, so can His true followers. Most of us can look at someone we know and love and discern when they are feeling physically ill. Such an ability is not considered remarkable in any way. Is it any more remarkable when Christians are sensitive to and concerned about the spiritual welfare of those around them? If you find it difficult, if not impossible, to discern Christians from non-Christians, you may wisely ask why. If you cannot tell when your brother or sister is in spiritual health, it may well be a mark of your own declension. Spiritual blindness marks many that claim the name of Jesus. Knowing virtually nothing of spiritual health themselves, they find it impossible to perceive the spiritual sickness of their own immediate world. Such weakness is unknown to Jesus, the Great Physician. When you cannot see signs of declension around you and you cannot hear the cries of the perishing multitudes, you need to look to your own spiritual welfare.

23. When you are willing to cheat your employer, backsliding is apparent. Every employee owes his employer full measure. If the hours of employment are 8:00 to 4:30, these are designated to be the hours of labor. Mere presence on the premises during these hours is hardly sufficient. If one is hired to work forty hours per week, that means forty hours of actual productive employment, not merely forty hours, more or less, on the job site. Obviously, office supplies, tools, equipment, and materials provided at work are not for home and personal use. Christians know these things and earnest believers take such responsibilities seriously. It is inconceivable that a true follower of Jesus Christ would cheat his employer. Can you imagine Jesus cheating His Father in heaven while He was here on earth with a job to do?

The backslider doesn't seem to see it this way. He finds little difficulty coming to work late and leaving early. The backslider considers lunch and coffee breaks flexible, and if two or three hours a day are thus consumed, he has no inward struggles with dishonesty. Nor does visiting with other employees and disrupting their work stir the backslider to anguish. A little theft of time, a little theft of goods, "What's so unusual about that?" the backslider inquires. Being filled with his own ways, can he really be expected to concern himself with his employer's welfare?

24. When you find yourself rich in grace and mercy and marvel at your own godlikeness, then you have fallen far in your backsliding. Every true Christian is marked by spiritual humility. There is no way a growing Christian can conceive of himself as having *arrived.* Jesus spoke eloquently on this theme in the Sermon on the Mount: *Blessed are the poor in spirit: for theirs is the kingdom of heaven* (Matthew 5:3). Who are the poor in spirit but those who know how far they still have to go—those who, having seen God in His infinite majesty and holiness, realize how truly unlike God they are. While appreciative of every mercy received and every grace practiced, the poor in spirit are ever aware that the graces they lack are far more numerous than the grace they enjoy, and the mercy they show is nothing in comparison with the mercy they themselves experience. To His own word on the poor in spirit must be tied Jesus' word to those that mourn. They too are blessed or happy *for they shall be comforted* (Matthew 5:4). Those who mourn are those who, having seen God as He is, then see themselves as they are. What can the man who compares himself with God do but mourn? Somehow the backslider fails to perceive things this way, and that failure is overwhelming evidence of his tragic condition.

25. **When your tears are dried up and the hard, cold spiritual facts of your existence cannot unleash them, see this as an awful testimony both of the hardness of your heart and the depth of your backsliding.** If your prayerlessness does not cause the tears to flow, are you not being confronted with the evidence of your backsliding? If your own personal sin does not provoke you to tears, are you not being confronted with the hardness of your heart? If the decline of spiritual interest all around you is both unnoticed and unalarming and totally incapable of forcing tears from your eyes, is it not because of your backslidden condition? If the lostness of your own children, your parents, your sisters, your husband, your wife, your brothers, your neighbors, your friends, your schoolmates and your companions on the job cannot unleash the tears, is it not because you no longer really care for the very things that stir most deeply the heart of God? When the things that grieve the Saviour have no power to grieve you, do you not have clear evidence that you are in a backslidden condition? Jesus saw Jerusalem and He wept. Do you weep over your Jerusalem? When Jesus beheld the hardness of men's hearts, His own heart was broken. Is yours? Surely no more certain sign of backsliding could possibly exist than an inability to weep with the Son of God and an unwillingness to share His heartbreak.

If any of these aspects of backsliding apply to you, do not lose heart. Ask, how did I get into such a backslidden condition? Did it happen overnight? Is it the result of one single moment of carelessness? Was it caused by a solitary sin? No, this would be highly unlikely. Usually backsliding happens a little bit at a time. Let me illustrate. It is rush hour in the New York City subway. Here's the picture: the train is crowded and no seats remain. There is, however, a three or four inch space between you and the person on your right. An aggressive passenger, unwilling to stand, spies the narrow gap and sits down— mostly on you and your neighbor. With a few bold wiggles the newcomer manages to force himself into a place a more timid soul would have never considered possible. So it is with the sins that lead to backsliding. Your life as a Christian is seemingly full of Christ and there is no room for self, but an aggressive sin comes and wiggles its way into your life, crowding Christ out just a little bit. You give place to this sin and soon another does the same thing. Eventually, your life is no longer filled with Christ but with backsliding. Sin by sin, error by error, selfishness by selfishness, the backsliding continues until you are virtually empty of Christ and full of sin and self.

When is a revival needed? Revival is never more needed than when signs of backsliding appear. Revival is never more needed than when backsliding surrounds the church, permeating its ministries and destroying its effectiveness. Revival is never more needed than when millions of professing Christians are marked with tragic signs of spiritual decline and the evidence of their backsliding rises as an awful stench in the nostrils of God. Revival is never more needed than when a church supposes itself victorious on the front lines of battle, but in reality all around it lie the scarred corpses of the victims of its backsliding. Revival is needed when the backslider is filled with his own ways.

Like Jeremiah and ourselves, Hosea lived in days of backsliding. He likened the sliding back of the Israelites to a backslidden heifer (Hosea 4:16) and lamented the weakness of God's people in backsliding (11:7). In drawing his prophecy to its close, Hosea urged, *O Israel, return unto the LORD thy God; for thou hast fallen by thine iniquity. Take with you words, and turn to the LORD: say unto Him, Take away all iniquity, and receive us graciously....* And God responded saying, *I will heal their backsliding, I will love them freely; for mine anger is turned away from him* (14:1,2,4).

When professing Christians are filled with their own ways and backsliding is evident everywhere, it is definitely time to pray in the words of Habakkuk: *O LORD, revive Thy work in the midst of the years, in the midst of the years make known; in wrath remember mercy* (3:2b).

Chapter Three

When
Can
Revival
Be
Expected?

We must be very earnest and importunate in our prayers to God and persevere in them till we obtain the mercy we pray for. For to be cold and formal in any prayer to God is to invite denial from Him. And therefore, in such a case, to hope for an answer of peace is the most daring presumption. And for this reason, fervency is made an essential qualification of such prayers as are acceptable to God through Jesus Christ.... And indeed, when we consider with whom we have to do in prayer, and of how great importance it is that we should attain the answer of our requests, and more especially when we are praying for such a comprehensive blessing as the reviving of God's work, we may easily be convinced that we can never be too earnest in our supplication to God on this occasion. And agreeably, when we look into the Holy Scriptures and meet with any account of the saints praying to God, we shall find either in the prayer itself, if it be recorded there, or in the general account that is given of it, that they were in a flame of devotion and offered up their petitions to heaven with a greatest ardency of soul.... And therefore, if we would succeed in our supplications to God for so important a blessing as this of reviving the work of God, we must be frequent and fervent in our prayers to God for it and if we do not presently see the success of these prayers we must not be discouraged and give over the duty, but we must humbly resolve with holy Jacob in his wrestling with the angel of the Lord, that we will not let Him alone until He blesses us. That is, we must persevere in the duty and cry to God with all possible importunity, until we find the Holy Spirit reviving His own work both in ourselves and in others. And if God does but once open and enlarge our hearts to pray to Him with this persevering importunity, we need not doubt the success of our prayers, for God can as soon deny Himself as deny an answer to the fervent prayers of His people.

John Webb, Boston, Massachusetts

When Can Revival Be Expected?

In many ordinary matters of life it is possible to anticipate results. If a frugal person carefully invests a significant portion of his income throughout his working life, he can ordinarily anticipate retirement with some sense of security. If a homeowner plants, sprinkles and fertilizes a lawn in the early spring, he can usually mow it all summer. If an employee works faithfully from day to day, he can probably expect a return on payday. If a market-stall owner displays luscious fruit, properly priced, in the morning, he can normally hope to count the money in his pocket that evening. If a mother fills the home with the fragrance of a delicious supper, she well knows there will be dirty dishes to wash soon thereafter.

Seed time and harvest follow predictable schedules. Before the farmer can expect the harvest there are certain things he must do: he must prepare the ground, plant the seeds and cultivate as necessary. The farmer knows, however, that he cannot germinate the seeds, cause the plants to grow or produce the increase. If the harvest is to come, God must provide the sunshine and the rain. The farmer and the Lord, working harmoniously together according to known patterns, produce the ordinary harvest.

The farmer could foolishly say, *Because I cannot do it all, I will do nothing.* He could spend the days of spring and summer in his rocking chair declaring, *God alone can give the increase.* But no matter how fervent his declaration of God's ability may be, that farmer will reap no autumn harvest off his fields.

Equally as foolish is the declaration of the farmer who says, *I am a self-made man. All that I have I have gained by my own hard work.* Let him bend his back to the toil from dawn to dark, if the God he denies withholds the sunshine and the rain, this man's fields will know no more of harvest than those of the slothful. It is the cooperative effort of man with God that keeps food on our tables.

In the minds of some, revival follows this same agricultural pattern. They declare that revival is the joint work of God and man. They inform us, *If men do all they can, God will send the harvest in the form of revival.* If asked the question, *Why are revivals so rare?* they quickly respond by saying, *We do not have revival because we do not want revival badly enough to pay the full price.* By this theory, the right use of the right means will produce the desired results. As the farmer must prepare the soil, plant the seed and cultivate the growing crops, so according to this notion, the Church must prepare the earth, sow the seed of the Word of God and cultivate professing Christians so that the harvest of revival may come.

If you are prepared to define revival as ordinary harvest, you may be ready to embrace this viewpoint. I have been urging you, however, to see revival as an extraordinary result or an extraordinary harvest. Why then do some insist that the principles governing ordinary Christian work also govern revival?

Certainly the body of Christ is required to approach its task in the world with the same earnest willingness and hard work as the farmer. By all means, the Church should be as faithful in fulfilling all of its responsibilities as the Lord is in fulfilling His. Unquestionably, it is the joint work of the Spirit of God with the people of God which moves the Church forward from harvest to harvest, decade after decade, century upon century. But this is ordinary, precious, wonderful gospel work.

Revival is not ordinary gospel work. Revival does not fall into the seasonal pattern of planting and harvesting. God, in His own mercy, has in special seasons granted harvests that seem to have no direct relationship to the ordinary day-in, day-out work of His Church. This special harvest of revival is needed today.

We must thank God for every ordinary work and every ordinary Christian worker in the world today. We need to thank Him for all the ordinary results these earnest workers are seeing as they enjoy the ordinary benefits of the Holy Spirit touch upon their labors. But because we are not living in ordinary days and because ordinary work is not accomplishing what desperately needs to be accomplished in this hour, we must concern ourselves deeply with the extraordinary work of the Holy Spirit in revival.

When can revival be expected? If revival is the extraordinary movement of the Holy Spirit, it can be expected when the sovereign God of the universe sends it. And when is God likely to send an extraordinary work? At a time of extraordinary need when His people are in the grip of extraordinary desire and when nothing short of an extraordinary outpouring of the Holy Spirit will satisfy.

THE EXTRAORDINARY NEED

God can be expected to send revival when an extraordinary need exists. Needs exist on various levels: political, economic, moral and spiritual.

1. Consider the political climate of our world. The entire world appears to be in the midst of political unrest. The prospect of worldwide war has scarcely ever been greater. The destructive potential of such conflict is almost beyond imagination. If international war does not destroy the western nations, they seem determined to accomplish that same end by self-destruction.

It is as if a spirit of madness has been unleashed. Try to rationally explain all that is going on and time after time you will be forced to shake your head in amazement. In a world that claims to be getting smarter with each passing generation, the proof is constantly before us that the basic human lessons of 5,000 years ago are still to be learned.

As *nations rage against nations,* and whole sectors of the world threaten to annihilate their opponents, misdirected science continues to provide the technology for this cataclysm. While apparently helpless in solving human problems, the geniuses of the world seem amazingly adept at discovering new methods for destroying one another.

A truly trusted politician is nearly as scarce these days as thirty-five pound gold nuggets. If a politician does not have his hand in the till at the moment, a large portion of the populations expects it is because he is just lifting his neighbor's wallet. Power seesaws back and forth and politicians come and go, but corruption in high places flourishes like spring flowers.

So malignant is the evil that once seemingly good men now declare, *If you can't lick them, join them.* Those who once paid their oppressive taxes with silent groans now seek questionable loopholes, while others, weary of seeing their hard-earned tax dollars squandered on political licentiousness, perpetrate outright dishonest tax evasion.

When every possible analysis of our political situation is made, when all the pros and cons of every issue are debated to a standstill, when every politician is weighed in the balances, the marshalled facts declare with ever increasing intensity the political bankruptcy of our world. What else do we require to convince us of the extraordinary need for revival?

2. Consider the economic climate of our world. There was a time when financial woes were considered the problem of a nation to be dealt with and resolved on a domestic level. But who can suppose that the economic distresses of our day can be resolved merely on a national level? With a large portion of the world in the midst of economic turmoil, what can one single nation do to bring its own financial house in order?

Has there ever been a time in the history of the world to compare with this present moment? Worldwide inflation rampages. The savings of a lifetime of hard work and thrift can be reduced to the value of a single loaf of bread by a decision made on the opposite side of the earth. Nations that have known almost nothing but poverty are suddenly rich while others who have gloried in their wealth for centuries are floundering and may soon be begging for mere subsistence.

Some people in our society foolishly contend that all the wrongs can be righted with a few more rules and regulations. Others, insisting that the origin of our economic woes is excessive government interference with private enterprise, believe that the lifting of restraints will cure the ills. As each, according to his own understanding, seeks to manipulate fiscal affairs to produce his envisioned solution, decay and panic increase on every hand.

In such days of economic turmoil no one can safely predict his own economic future. Prosperity may be just around the corner. The West may be on the verge of its greatest growth or its greatest disaster. In facing the hard, cold facts of world economics, we can know only one thing for certain: the opportunists will turn it to their best advantage if they can, even if the rest of the world perishes. No matter what tentative analysis is made of the worldwide economic chaos, one truth stands head and shoulders above all others: human greed is at its root. If this does not constitute an extraordinary need for revival, what does?

3. Consider the moral climate of the world. What has human pride done for us? If we can believe our analysts, no other generation that ever lived on earth has been as wise as ours. We are told that we have gained more knowledge in fifty years than has been gathered in all of previous history. So far *advanced* is our culture that it seems unthinkable to modern man to allow his life to be regulated by moral principles laid down thousands of years ago. Moses may have needed the Ten Commandments for the control of the ignorant savages of his day, but what have such outdated regulations to do with our *highly developed* society?

Subjectivism has taken the place of the fixed principles of moral law. Instead of judging conduct on the basis of God's dictates, we now ask, "Does it feel good?" and "Will I enjoy it?" and "Does it hurt the other person?" By such standards, every man is free to decide for himself what is right and wrong in any given situation. Well-meaning individuals insist, *Let your conscience be your guide.* So benighted are the advocates of open morality that they completely fail to realize that a seared or corrupt conscience can never be relied upon to guide its owner to do right. Having laid aside the moral boundaries fixed by our Maker, modern man has become bogged down in the filthy swamp of iniquity into which he has wandered.

If a young person declares himself on the side of old-fashioned morality, he may expect not only the jeers of friends, but also the scorn of teachers and possibly even of his own parents.

Moral corruption has been rife at other periods in the world's history, but during some of these times there was at least a church with high standards ready to speak against the surrounding wickedness and to hold high the banner of biblical morality. In our day the church itself shows increasing signs of moral corruption. If there is any difference between the fornication rate, the adultery rate, the divorce rate or the abortion rate in the church and the world it is scarcely discernable. Beyond doubt, the world now has vastly more influence on the church for evil than the church has on the world for good.

Hollywood entertainers are not the only ones using television to line their dens of iniquity with gold leaf. More than a few television preachers have padded their pockets with the donations of a gullible religious public. There appear to be individuals in all phases of religious work who are serving themselves and not God. Moral earnestness is hardly the earmark of all religious leaders. Personal purity has made few famous. Sexual looseness, once so strongly denounced by the church, now sits comfortably in padded pews. Most men in the pulpit readily discover that their parishioners are not nearly as serious about *the solemn vows they have taken* as the church covenant would lead outsiders to believe.

Justice and mercy are the great cries of our day, yet in the name of justice our courts regularly release the guilty to mercilessly plunder and violate the innocent. Millions lock themselves in their houses at night, fearing even to walk their dogs, lest their homes be invaded in their absence. In our determination to be broad-minded, moral reprobates hold positions of leadership and influence in schools, government, businesses and churches. Sins once considered so heinous that good men would scarcely name them are now portrayed vividly on television screens, in movie theatres and upon the pages of our mass-circulation magazines. To raise even a feeble voice of objection against pornography, violence and human degradation and perversion is to be branded a bigot, an obstructor of progress or an escapee from an old-fashioned asylum.

If the moral climate of our day does not reveal an extraordinary need for revival, what does?

4. Consider the spiritual climate. If we can believe the pollsters, upwards of fifty percent of all adult Americans have had a lasting *born-again* experience. In light of the political, economic and moral conditions around us, whatever does it mean to be a *born-again Christian?* Surely it cannot mean what some of us used to think. This precious term once referred to new life in God. The born-again had died to the life of sin, selfishness and injustice and had been resurrected anew in the likeness of Jesus Christ. Old things were described as having *passed away*; in the new birth, everything was declared new. So meaningless has this precious biblical term become that it is scarcely safe to use it without elaborate biblical definition and hedges.

Some churches seem filled with people who can tell you the day and the hour they accepted Christ but who live as if God were dead. So degenerate are our churches becoming, and so undisciplined by biblical truth, that young people are crying in heart agony, "Isn't there a genuine Christian somewhere whose godly life I can copy?"

Sadly, even many of our preachers seem determined to aid men in their apostasy. Timid and fearful public discourse is far more common than heart-searching, impassioned biblical preaching. If bold-faced heresy is not openly espoused in the pulpit, it is frequently taught in small classes. If Timothy needed Paul's warning, how much more do the preachers of our own day need to be told,

> *Preach the Word; be instant in season, out of season; reprove, rebuke, exhort with all longsuffering and doctrine. For the time will come when they will not endure sound doctrine; but after their own lusts shall they heap to themselves teachers, having itching ears; and they shall turn away their ears from the truth, and shall be turned unto fables* (Second Timothy 4:2-4).

Millions are seeking to use the precious cross of Jesus Christ as a fire escape from hell. While sailing through life unbroken, unrepentant and unyielded, these high-flying hypocrites call Jesus Christ *LORD*, while retaining mastery for themselves.

How many sermons today are preached by broken-hearted ministers who agonize over their congregations in prayer and strong pleadings? How many congregations are eager to hear the pure Word of God? Where do you find a people who *take heed how they hear* (Luke 8:18) with the kind of diligence that ought to characterize listeners everywhere? How many churches have their prayer rooms filled with eager supplicants crying to the Almighty for renewed spiritual blessings?

The typical church has its own spiritual status quo. While church norms vary from place to place, they are seldom high. In the typical congregation, let someone experience a great work of grace in his soul and become vocal in his praise of God and many hands will reach up to drag that person back down to the level of the congregation. Whereas Christians ought to work together to lift one another towards God, most local churches conspire to keep everyone in his place, lest the serenity, peace and quiet of a church in declension be disturbed.

The average church is more like a morgue than a hospital. There seem to be more Christians buried from churches than ever find life there. A genuine new convert in some churches would be rare enough to raise goose bumps on the pews.

There are professing Christians who do not know how to pray, how to witness or how to live a godly life. If hard pressed on any of these seemingly fundamental aspects of Christianity, they would be insulted and possibly even angry enough to change churches.

If personal holiness were made an absolute requirement for church membership in every Christian Church throughout the world, a massive reemployment program for tens of thousands of clergy would become an immediate necessity. Has God ever rescinded His demand, *Be ye holy, as I am holy?* Obviously not! And since He hasn't, what possible excuse will so many offer at the final judgment?

Without seeking to multiply evidence, have we not ample proof of spiritual declension? Can you personally feel it is only the other fellow who stands in need and not you yourself? If your own spiritual temperature and the spiritual climate of the church around you does not constitute an extraordinary need for revival, what does?

EXTRAORDINARY AWARENESS

God can be expected to send revival when these extraordinary needs are extraordinarily felt.

The mere existence of a need does not necessitate a feeling concerning it. People have died of curable diseases without even knowing they needed a physician. All the arrangements to maneuver a man out of his job can be made right under his nose without his realizing what is happening and instead of feeling the need to seek work elsewhere he can be erroneously supposing himself in enjoyment of a lifetime position at the very moment he is terminated. Students have flunked out of college without ever having felt any real need to study. Marriages have gotten all the way to the divorce courts before both partners realized there was trouble in the marriage. Men have lived serenely for seventy years on this earth and then slipped into an eternity of torment without ever feeling any serious need to seek God and prepare for their future.

It is even possible to agree with my analysis of the political, economic, moral and spiritual climate of our times without feeling any need of extraordinary divine intervention. One can reason that the world has been in trouble before and found its way out. Some who are prepared to concede that the times are bad are not yet ready to acknowledge that the times are impossible. If there is still something a person thinks he can do to save the day, he is unlikely to feel the need of any extraordinary measures. Even if he acknowledges that he can do nothing personally to turn the world around, he may have hopes that human kind itself, by mustering all its efforts, can still be its own savior. As long as there is one spark of hope left for deliverance by human hands, the great pressing needs of the hour may not be felt.

Doubtless, many feel the need but do not feel it in any extraordinary way. They may feel it only intermittently. Perhaps they feel it when they read the newspaper headlines or review the motion picture advertisements, but they are able to live long hours each day with no pressing sense of need. Perhaps the assassination of another public figure will prompt this sense of need, but after a while it may once again be forgotten.

Some make a deliberate effort not to feel the need too greatly. They pride themselves on their buoyant, cheerful spirits. Their friends may regard them as perpetual optimists. They are not used to carrying great burdens in their souls, and they have no desire to begin now.

Others may feel the need sporadically because the press of their own affairs—family, friends, business, recreation—prevents them from focusing on anything outside of themselves for more than brief periods.

Some, too, because of the nature of their perception of the spiritual world, are content to say, *Whatever will be, will be.* With that note of resignation, they are content to leave the whole matter in the hands of *fate.*

But can a truly caring Christian live in the midst of such needs without experiencing extraordinary feelings? Can the Christian see his brother oppressed and not care? Can the true believer see evil prevail and say, *Whatever will be, will be?* Can those who truly love Jesus keep their eyes focused on their own small world of self while anguish and misery prevail around them? Can the truly born-again let a buoyant, cheerful spirit prevent their feeling the crying needs of humanity?

The great question that needs to be asked is, "Does God Himself see this present world in great need?" If God sees the need and feels it, how can His children possibly remain insensitive. Remember, Jesus looked over the Jerusalem of His day and wept. Doesn't He weep over the political, financial, moral and spiritual chaos of our own day with an equally great anguish and concern? Isn't He again weeping over the hardheartedness of men? And doesn't the Savior, who loves us with an everlasting love, even now weep over our lack of extraordinary feelings concerning all these extraordinary needs which surround us?

When a band of earnest Christians comes under the terrific burden of felt needs, then, and not until then, will there be a glimmer of revival hope before us.

EXTRAORDINARY SENSE OF GOD

God can be expected to send revival when those extraordinary feelings of extraordinary need provoke an extraordinary sense of His presence.

While all is going well it is not uncommon to forget God. Countless people throughout the world do not bow before their Maker in adoration and praise even once a week. But when a man comes under the overwhelming burden of felt needs, his interest in God is wonderfully increased.

When our burdens are light and our strength is at full height, we will turn aside proffered help with pleasant ease. But if the burdens become more than our strength can bear, we will be glad enough for someone else's help.

Some years ago I was sent a shipment of some 10,000 old and rare books from Europe. Knowing the date of their anticipated arrival, my wife and I arranged to have friends help us unload them at our home. When the truck arrived at our door, we discovered that the three large wooden crates in which the books were packed weighed approximately four tons each and were placed in the van sideways. Thus it was impossible to open them on the end intended. With tremendous difficulty, we had to strip off tar-paper roofs and dismantle these well-made crates board by board. Two other difficulties added greatly to our labors. Our expected friends could devote only a few minutes helping us and the individual book boxes within the crates weighed approximately 150 pounds each. Hour by hour my wife and I labored over this seemingly impossible task. First one crate, then the second, and finally the third. Evening came and still we toiled on alone. The two of us: small, tired, but determined, finally wrestled that last box to the storage area and collapsed in total weariness. All that day we felt the need of help. Had even a stranger offered a hand, we would have grabbed it with delight. But while no human hands were raised to assist us in all that heavy labor, we knew in the midst of our felt needs the wonderful presence of our sustaining Lord. That day, for the first time in our lives, we truly understood and felt with delight the meaning of *As thy days, so shall thy strength be* (Deuteronomy 33:25b).

If the physical burdens of a day's labors are great enough to create an unusual awareness of the presence of God, ought we not to expect the extraordinary needs of the chaotic world around us to provoke an even greater and more blessed sense of God's presence?

When you know there is no way you can meet the extraordinary needs about you, when you are fully convinced that God and God alone can meet these needs, and when you realize that God not only can meet extraordinary needs but also desires to do exactly that, then

the sense of His presence becomes wonderfully apparent. As this
sense of God's presence grows, the awareness of the blessedness of
His presence grows with it. Whereas earlier you might have been
content with an occasional audience with the King of kings and Lord
of lords, you begin to delight in His presence and find it absolutely
indispensable. When this sense of the presence of God among His
people becomes truly extraordinary, let believers everywhere have the
faith to believe that a powerful revival is on its way.

EXTRAORDINARY SPIRIT OF PRAYER

God can be expected to send revival when this extraordinary sense of
His presence provokes an extraordinary spirit of believing prayer.

Both the quantity of prayer and the quality of prayer are wonderfully affected by one's sense of the presence of God. When God
seems distant and disinterested, prayer is dull and difficult. As the
presence of God becomes more and more real, the delight in His
presence and the courage to ask and expect great things increase.

Prayer is obviously a perfectly ordinary duty of every Christian.
Much praying, however, may be too ordinary. It is possible to pray by
rote like a machine, or to pray and within minutes forget the very
petitions offered. In James 1:5-8 a very severe warning is laid upon
us,

> *If any of you lack wisdom, let him ask of God, that giveth to all
> men liberally, and upbraideth not; and it shall be given him.
> But let him ask in faith, nothing wavering. For he that wavereth
> is like a wave of the sea driven with the wind and tossed. For
> let not that man think that he shall receive any thing of the
> Lord. A double minded man is unstable in all his ways.*

Much praying is characterized by double-mindedness. A petition is
made and then wavering occurs. In the context of this passage it is
clear that God may choose to answer a *rich man's* prayer for wisdom
by bringing him low, just as He may choose to answer the prayer of
the brother of *low degree* by exalting him. In either case, praying
persons are warned against wavering.

Wavering prayer for revival is hardly extraordinary. Some pray a
little for an outpouring of the Holy Spirit, but when God begins to
break them by chastening and affliction, they soon become double-
minded. They are glad enough to see a brother brought low, but are
hardly ready for such humiliation themselves. Let the wavering one
realize he will not receive *anything of the Lord.* God is ready to listen
to the prayers of those who have really decided what they want and
need, but not to the prayers of the vacillating. A young man, who had
been part of a revival prayer meeting, said to me one day, "I don't

know what to do. I have been praying for revival for a year and nothing has happened." When I asked him if he would be praying for revival a year hence he acted surprised and said he did not know. His surprise seemed even greater when I informed him that a major difference between himself and God was that God knew whether or not he would be praying for revival in future years, and that if he did not want revival badly enough to know he would keep praying for it until the answer came he should realize he was as a double-minded man with no right to expect to receive anything from the Lord.

Ordinary, dull, listless prayer can hardly be expected to bring down revival from heaven. *The effectual fervent prayer of a righteous man availeth much* (James 5:16b) but no such promise is made concerning heartless, careless petitions. All revival praying should be characterized by fervency. To be anything other than fervent in praying for revival is to acknowledge before the Almighty a spirit of indifference in the face of crushing needs.

Prayer on the run can certainly not be described as extraordinary, albeit it appears to be the only kind of prayer some professed Christians know. An occasional moment of bowing the head may have its place and benefit, but is not fully in keeping with the pressing needs of the hour of present crisis. Earnest seasons of protracted prayer—when everything else is laid aside and the heart of the supplicant is laid bare before the mighty God—constitute extraordinary prayer, the kind which the great pressing need for revival demands.

Did you ever try to pray when your heart was stone cold toward God? Can men be expected to turn to earnest prayer because they are exhorted to do so? Can earnestness in prayer be forged by human effort? Can a prayerless heart prevail before the throne of grace by sheer determination?

There is a natural link between extraordinary prayer and an extraordinary sense of the presence of God. To commune at great length with the God whose presence is wonderfully known is not difficult. To ask courageously for large and important blessings is hardly unthinkable when Christ's presence is felt among His people. Those who know Christ best realize He delights in their prayers. They know He is not offended by their zeal and earnestness or troubled by their frequent pleadings. They know He does not grow weary of their continual asking or require new and clever ways to express the desires of the heart. They know it isn't even necessary to formulate in human words the burden of their souls. They know He cares, and because He cares, He delights in their dependence upon Him.

That prayer which lays hold upon God and declares, *I will not let you go until you bless me,* is now, as it was in the days of Jacob, the prayer that delights the Father's heart.

When prayers and strong pleas for revival are made to God both day and night, when the children of God find they can no longer tolerate the absence of revival blessing, when extraordinary seeking of an extraordinary outpouring becomes extraordinarily earnest, and when the burden of prayer for revival becomes almost unbearable, then let praying hearts take courage for the Spirit of God who is the Spirit of revival has brought His people to this place for His purpose.

EXTRAORDINARY GLORY TO GOD

When the answer to those extraordinary prayers is sure to result in extraordinary glory to God, true revival may be expected.

God can be counted on to send revival only when there is a people prepared to give Him all the glory. He reveals Himself as a jealous God who will not share His glory with another. The very first commandment underlines this truth in unmistakable language. Israel's greatest offense against her God was in her repeated failure to give Him all the glory due His name.

No sin can be expected to cause the withdrawal of divine blessing sooner than the grievous sin of compromising God's glory. Families come to ruin when the glory of God is forgotten. Churches become as desolate wildernesses when God's jealousy is provoked. Entire nations fall when the glory which belongs to the Eternal One is misappropriated. Surely God will not send revival to a people unprepared to guard His glory. If men must share the glory of a revival among themselves, there will be no extraordinary movement of the Spirit of God in their midst.

While men remain convinced they can save themselves, they are hardly prepared to give all the glory of their salvation to God. If the conviction prevails that revival comes when men do their part, those very men who consider themselves as having done their part may expect to share the glory. Revival will not come under such circumstances. When God sends revival to His people, He wants it clearly understood that it is His doing and not theirs.

Some may be prepared to pray earnestly for revival, fearing that if revival does not come, their very way of life will be destroyed by the increasing corruption on every hand. Others may lift their hearts toward God in revival prayer when they see their bank accounts threatened and retirement security vanishing before their eyes. Still others may be grieved for loved ones living in sin and find this the motivation for revival praying. But let it be clearly understood, worthy as these and similar concerns may be, the glory of God is the great overwhelming reason for earnest revival praying.

What could add more to the glory of God than an outpouring of the Holy Spirit at this time? Picture millions of newly revived Christians gathered before the Saviour's throne, singing and rejoicing and praising God with all their hearts for the wonderful mercies of His reviving grace. Add to this picture countless numbers of genuine new converts drawn into the Kingdom of Christ by this very divine outpouring. Broaden the picture to include churches by the thousands filled with the power of the Holy Spirit, their breaches of brother-hood healed, the impurity of their doctrines purged by the Spirit of Truth, the profaneness of their worship sanctified and the glory of God their single objective. Stand next to a revived pastor and see the thrill he is experiencing in serving a revived people. Sense his delight in the glory of God and his worship of the Mighty One who has brought the revival to pass. See the Lord of heaven smiling down upon a revived earth. These are reasons enough to storm the throne of God with extraordinary prayer for extraordinary help in meeting extraordinary needs.

Chapter Four

What
Truth
Must
Revival
Emphasize?

You may be very sorry for your sin because it may fix a scandal upon your character, because it may have injured your temporal estate, or because it may ruin you in the eternal world...and yet know nothing of true repentance. True repentance is a more kindly, generous thing: it proceeds from an affecting sense of the baseness and malignity of sin in itself. Sin appears to the true penitent as some sort of poison to us. That is, not only hateful because it is deadly and destructive, but hateful and nauseous in itself. I do not mean that the fear of punishment is no ingredient in true repentance: the love of God and self love are very consistent if the latter is kept in due subordination to the former; and therefore the fear of punishment has great weight even with the evangelical penitent. What I mean is that the fear of punishment is not the principal, much less the only spring and motive of true repentance. The true penitent hates sin even when he is not thinking of heaven or hell, but only viewing it in its own nature. If he were allowed to go to heaven in the ways of sin, he would by no means choose it. Heaven itself would be less acceptable to him if it were the end of such a course.

Samuel Davies, Princeton, New Jersey

What Truth Must Revival Emphasize?

What urgent note characterized apostolic preaching but is scarcely heard in the church today? Why, of course, repentance! Time after time throughout the New Testament the call to repentance was sounded. The preaching of John the Baptist was dominated by this theme. With it he opened and closed his ministry. For the cause of repentance he lived and died. The mandatory nature of repentance was woven throughout the entire fabric of the life and ministry of Jesus Himself and its urgent necessity repeatedly proclaimed. The Church began, according to the Book of Acts, with earnest calls to repentance and with severe warnings against those who refused to heed the call. At no time throughout the entire New Testament does this dominant theme disappear. Even the Revelation of Jesus Christ given to John on the Isle of Patmos focused on the urgent necessity of repentance in five of the seven letters sent to the Churches of Asia. From beginning to end, the plain demand of the New Testament is *repent or perish!*

Why is so little heard on this subject in our day? How can we explain the existence of so many professing Christians in our churches who are not repentant? How can so many ministers justify their failure to make earnest calls to repentance a constant theme in their preaching when both the New Testament requires it and the lives of their people demonstrate its need?

With spiritual declension on every hand, with moral corruption rolling over the nation like a tidal wave, can there be any biblical doctrine more needed now than repentance?

What is repentance? Is it a passing feeling of remorse or guilt which causes a person to say, "I'm sorry"? Certainly many professing Christians have felt this. Can tears and a feeling of shame over sins committed answer to the biblical call to repentance? Or can even an apology to the Almighty be equated with this New Testament doctrine?

Is repentance a change of mind toward sin? Untold numbers of professing Christians have experienced a change of mind. At one time they were indifferent toward their conduct and unaware of the gulf that separated them from God. But then they realized sin was a

problem to them personally and came face to face with the fact that
the end result of sin was eternal separation from God. The prospect
of hell was frightening, and rather than face it for eternity, they
changed their mind about sin. No longer could they feel indifference
toward their lifelong build-up of accumulated evil. They needed a
Saviour and called upon Jesus. The guilt of their sins seemed lifted,
and they happily acknowledged themselves Christians. Is this
repentance?

Can penance or an act of self-abasement or mortification of the
flesh be described as repentance? Did John the Baptist call the
people of his day to contrition? Is punishment of self in keeping with
the call of Jesus Christ to repentance? Isn't it possible to do penance
and yet never repent? Can not one clothe himself in sackcloth and
ashes without ever meeting the New Testament requirement of
repentance?

If repentance is more than remorse, more than a change of mind,
more than penance, what then is it?

REPENTANCE—AN ONGOING PROCESS

First and foremost, repentance is not any single thought or act.
Repentance is not something once done and forever accomplished.
Repentance is an ongoing process. One must be forever repentant. It
is not enough to have once felt sorrow over sin. No single change of
mind will suffice. No individual act of self-abasement will meet the
biblical requirement. True repentance affects the whole man, alters
the entire lifestyle and does not cease.

In genuine biblical repentance one does not merely seek to escape
the wrath of God or the guilt of conscience. The repentant person
turns from all that displeases God toward that which pleases Him.
The repentant individual turns his back upon sin and himself and in
faith turns to Jesus Christ. This turning from sin and self toward
Christ is and must be a continuing process. It is not enough to have
once turned from sin toward Christ. The turning is a day-by-day,
year-after-year process of refusing to follow sin and self and of
deliberately following Christ.

The truly penitent will be able to say not just "I repented," but "I
am repentant!"

REPENTANCE—AN ABOUT-FACE

Biblical repentance is a permanent change of direction. Think of a
person walking one way. He realizes he is going where he does not
wish to be, turns around completely, and goes in the opposite
direction. Everyone starts out life going the wrong way. By his very
nature, man is a sinner on his way to destruction. Every sin and

selfish act places the sinner closer to his eternal destination. In repentance, he experiences a complete about-face. Turning toward heaven, Christ and righteousness, the repentant individual begins to move with new purpose and resolve in the right direction.

How far can a person go who walks a mile east, turns about and walks a mile west, turns again and goes two miles east and then turns once more and goes two miles west? Obviously, not very far! So too, if a person abandons sin and self one day but turns back to it the next, there is no convincing evidence of repentance having occurred. True biblical repentance is known to exist when a person sets his face like a flint toward the City of God and no temptations toward sin and self are sufficient to cause him to abandon his steady march toward God.

When revival comes, this genuine biblical doctrine of repentance will be restored to its rightful place in our churches and in the lives of professing Christians.

REPENTANCE—A GIFT FROM GOD

True repentance is a gift from God. In the days of the second persecution (Acts 5), the Apostles were commanded by the Jewish leaders not to preach or teach in the name of Jesus. But Peter and others declared with vehemence,

> *We ought to obey God rather than men. The God of our fathers raised up Jesus, whom ye slew and hanged on a tree. Him hath God exalted with His right hand to be a Prince and a Savior, for* **to give repentance to Israel, and forgiveness of sins** (verses 29-31).

Please lay hold of this blessed truth: God gave repentance and forgiveness of sins to Israel.

Repentance was also God's gift to the Gentiles. In his vindication of his ministry to them (Acts 11), the Apostle Peter described his vision of the great sheet let down from heaven by four corners and his subsequent ministry among the Gentiles in Caesarea:

> *As I began to speak, the Holy Ghost fell on them, as on us at the beginning. Then remembered I the word of the Lord, how that He said, John indeed baptized with water; but ye shall be baptized with the Holy Ghost. Forasmuch then as God gave them the like gift as He did unto us, who believed on the Lord Jesus Christ; what was I, that I could withstand God? When they [the Apostles and brethren in Jerusalem] heard these things, they held their peace, and glorified God, saying, Then hath God also to the Gentiles* **granted repentance unto life**

(verses 15-18).

Marvel with Peter and the brethren in the realization that God gave the gift of repentance to the Gentiles just as He had to the Jews.

Paul, being very much aware that true repentance is a gift of God, counseled Timothy to build his ministry upon this same awareness:

> *Flee also youthful lusts: but follow righteousness, faith, charity, peace, with them that call on the Lord out of a pure heart. But foolish and unlearned questions avoid, knowing that they do gender strifes. And the servant of the Lord must not strive; but be gentle unto all men, apt to teach, patient, in meekness instructing those that oppose themselves;* **if God peradventure will give them repentance to the acknowledging of the truth; and that they may recover themselves out of the snare of the devil, who are taken captive by him at his will** (Second Timothy 2:22-26).

No one truly repents on his own. Genuine repentance is always the gift of God.

Our churches suffer not only from a lack of teaching and preaching on repentance, but also from the failure to adequately realize God's place in this doctrine. Did you ever pray that God would give you the required and wonderful gift of repentance? If you teach or preach the Word of God, have you prayed earnestly and consistently that your public ministry would be accompanied by the gift of repentance? In praying for your church and the outreach of the Gospel, do you pray constantly that the gift of repentance will accompany all acts and labors, all ministries and services?

To describe repentance as a gift of God may seem to provide an excuse for unrepentant persons. They have only to claim nonreceipt of the gift to be excused from its obligations. The New Testament teaching on repentance, however, leaves the sinner completely without excuse. God wills that all men should come to repentance (Second Peter 3:9). All men everywhere are commanded by their Maker to repent (Acts 17:30). God works graciously in the lives of individuals, prompting repentance by His goodness (Romans 2:4). Jesus warns, *Except ye repent, ye shall all likewise perish* (Luke 13:3,5).

In his final commission to His followers, Jesus commanded that repentance and remission of sins should be preached in His name among all nations, beginning at Jerusalem (Luke 24:47). This command has never been rescinded. God gives the gift of repentance but men are commanded to preach it. God gives the gift of repentance but men and women must act when God speaks. Any failure to receive this gift and to act upon it only intensifies a person's guilt before God. Let no man say, "I cannot repent," while God is willingly giving an enabling gift of repentance. The issue is not, **can** men repent? but **will** men repent?

REPENTANCE FROM DEAD WORKS

The biblical demand for repentance is in two separate and distinct areas: repentance from sin and repentance from dead works. You say, "I have repented!" Have you repented of all your sins? You say, "I have repented!" Have you repented of all your dead works?

In summarizing the wonderful difference between the Old Covenant and the New Covenant, the author of the Book of Hebrews contrasts the effectiveness of the shedding of blood. Under the Old Covenant the blood of bulls and of goats and the sprinkling of the ashes of a heifer symbolically purified the flesh (9:13). That is to say, the sacrificial system of the Old Testament was itself external and produced external results. A ceremonially unclean person was ostracized from the assembly of the people, but through a proper sacrifice or offering could be restored to normal life. Under the New Covenant, however, the effect of shed blood is far from external. Ponder this biblical question, *How much more shall the blood of Christ, who through the eternal Spirit offered Himself without spot to God, purge your conscience from dead works to serve the living God?* (9:14). The blood of Christ affects the inner man. It is the conscience that it purges. But did you ever wonder why the issue in this passage is *dead works* and not *sin*? Why are we not told here that the blood of Christ purges the conscience from *sin*? What does it mean to have the conscience purged from *dead works*?

In considering this tremendous question, let us remind ourselves of an earlier passage in this same epistle. At the end of the fifth chapter of Hebrews the author declares he has many things to say (verse 11ff) which are hard to be uttered because of the dullness of hearing of those to whom he writes. In warm, but urgent tones, he reminds them that, while they ought to be teachers, they still need to be taught the *first principles of the oracles of God*. While they ought to be able to digest the strong meat of the Word of God, they are still so unskillful in the *word of righteousness* that they must be fed with milk like babes. To cater to their lower instincts and to encourage them in their slovenly spiritual ways is absolutely contrary to the purpose of the epistle. Thus the author states his unwillingness to deal again with the first principles of Christianity and after mentioning them in passing, goes on to warn, in the severest possible language, those who are not pressing on to perfection (6:4-12). Consider, please, what he lays down as foundational principles: 1. Repentance from dead works; 2. Faith toward God; 3. Baptisms; 4.

Laying on of hands; 5. Resurrection of the dead; and 6. Eternal judgment (Hebrews 6:1,2).

Did you notice that first foundational principle: repentance from dead works? I put it to you bluntly: are you aware that repentance from dead works is a first principle of Christianity? Need I remind you now that it is repentance from dead works and not merely repentance from sin that is here declared foundational?

Have you ever repented of dead works? Has your conscience been purged from them so that you might serve the living God? It is evident that if these questions are to be answered with integrity, we must understand what dead works are and what repentance from them involves.

DEAD WORKS DEFINED

First, any religious act calculated to gain merit with God by human effort is a dead work. Worship can be dead work. Prayer can be dead work. Hymn singing can be dead work. Tithing can be dead work. Deeds of kindness can be dead works. Accepting Jesus Christ can be dead work. Fasting can be dead work. Preaching can be dead work. R. C. H. Lenski wrote:

> Some think that "dead" means "sinful" works in general. These certainly would be dead weight on the conscience. Yet here [Hebrews 9:14] as well as in Hebrews 6:1, "dead works" are scarcely crimes and flagrant breaches of law but rather all formal, empty, false legal observances and self-invented works whereby men would seek to stand before God.[1]

It is possible to turn any act of worship, devotion or service into a dead work.

Consider this shocking fact: large numbers of persons can tell you the very day and hour they accepted Christ as their personal Savior but live as if they belong to the devil rather than to God. Many professing Christians even believe it is possible to accept Christ as Savior while rejecting Him as Lord. Evangelists and pastors have frequently taught people this possibility. It is not uncommon to hear a public invitation at the end of a service phrased somewhat as follows:

> I appeal to all who have never received Christ as their Savior to accept Him now. Will you respond? Please raise your hand. Now I want to speak to those of you who have already received

---

[1]R. C. H. Lenski, *The Interpretation of the Epistle to the Hebrews.* Minneapolis: Augsburg Publishing House, 1966, p. 300.

Christ as your Savior and are sure that you are on your way to heaven. You know that you have not yet received Christ as your Lord. Are you willing to accept Him as your Lord tonight? Please raise your hand.

Do these words sound familiar to you? They suggest a whole new doctrine—a two-phase salvation which allows a person to be rescued from hell by accepting Christ as a fire escape and then, if desired, a second option of being rescued from sin and self by yielding to Jesus Christ as Lord.

Where, in the entire New Testament, can a doctrine like this be found? Did the Lord Jesus Christ ever tell people He would save them from hell while they still retained control of their own lives? His very own words thunder against such nonsense: *Why call ye Me, Lord, Lord, and do not the things which I say?* (Luke 6:46); *Not every one that saith unto Me, Lord, Lord, shall enter into the kingdom of heaven; but he that doeth the will of My Father which is in heaven* (Matthew 7:21); and *No man can serve two masters: for either he will hate the one, and love the other; or else he will hold to the one, and despise the other. Ye cannot serve God and mammon* (Matthew 6:24).

Accepting Jesus Christ as Savior has become for millions of professing Christians nothing but a dead work. For many of them there has been no turning from sin and self and no yielding to the Lord Jesus Christ. Without genuine repentance there can be no genuine conversion. The true Christian has the life of God in him. This life is received by exchange: a life for a life—His life for my life. When I come to the end of myself and in faith surrender to Him, casting all upon Him, He replaces my broken and ruined life with His own life. Christ does not give life to those already satisfied with the life they have. It is impossible to have Christ as Saviour but not as Lord. One cannot be saved from hell without being saved from sin and self. To pretend otherwise is hypocrisy. To teach otherwise is heresy.

An excellent illustration of what it means to follow Christ as a dead work is found in chapter six of the Gospel of John. The passage opens with the declaration that Christ went over the Sea of Galilee and a crowd followed Him because they saw His miracles and were impressed. Jesus went up into a mountain with His disciples to teach, but in glancing up, He saw the great crowd coming once more. Jesus asked Philip about feeding the multitude and by a wonderful miracle did so with five barley loaves and two small fishes brought by a mere lad. Jesus then perceived that the crowd planned to take Him by force and make Him a king, so He slipped away to Capernaum. The crowd eagerly followed Him there also. Jesus, knowing exactly what was in their hearts, said, *Verily, verily, I say unto you, Ye seek me, not because ye saw the miracles, but because ye did eat of the loaves, and were filled. Labor not for the meat which perisheth, but for that meat which endureth unto everlasting life, which the Son of man shall give unto you: for Him hath God the Father sealed* (John 6:26,27).

That this crowd had been laboring for meat that perishes is evident in the amount of energy they spent chasing Jesus from place to place. In response to His demand, the people inquired, *What shall we do, that we might work the works of God?* Jesus replied, *This is the work of God, that ye believe on Him whom He hath sent* (verses 28,29). Although they had been following Him zealously, instead of now declaring their belief, they skirted the issue, saying, *What sign showest Thou then, that we may see, and believe Thee? What dost Thou work? (verse 30).* If it were not so tragic, we might almost laugh. They had already seen miracle after miracle, but when commanded to believe that Jesus Christ is the Lord God, they asked for yet another miracle. What is really in their hearts is revealed in verse 31, *Our fathers did eat manna in the desert; as it is written, He gave them bread from heaven to eat.* They were saying, in other words, "Jesus, as long as you feed us free bread and give us what we want, we will follow you, but don't lay any claims of Lordship upon us." Jesus then turned their request for bread into a beautiful unfolding of His true nature—the Bread come down from heaven. However, it was bread for the belly, not bread for the soul, that really interested this crowd. The chapter closes with the revelation that from that time many of Jesus' disciples went back and walked with Him no more. When Jesus asked the Twelve if they would go away also, Peter, who was just beginning to grasp the difference between dead works and living faith, declared, *Lord, to whom shall we go? Thou hast the words of eternal life. And we believe and are sure that Thou art that Christ, the Son of the living God* (verses 68,69).

Many obviously followed Jesus for what they hoped to get out of Him. These poor Jews loved free bread and were ready to receive it all the time, but they did not love the truth and were not willing to have it laid on them continually. As long as they got what they wanted without price and obligation, they were greatly interested. When the demands of faith and submission were laid down, however, their enthusiasm for Jesus fled rapidly.

Are there not many in our churches today who have accepted Christ for what they can get out of Him? They don't want to be forever lost and so they accept Christ as Savior. Let me emphasize the words *they accept Christ.* This is something they do, and having done it, they suppose that God is now in their debt and under their obligation. God cannot send them to hell, they think. After all, they have accepted Christ. They have not yielded to his Lordship or really believed what He says, but they still consider themselves safe because of what they have done. May I remind you again that anything man does to gain merit or favor with God is a dead work!

For millions, accepting Christ is every bit as much a dead work as was clamoring for free bread. Is there really any significant spiritual difference between seeking to use Christ for free food and seeking to use Christ as an escape from future danger? Jesus told those seeking bread, *This is the work of God, that ye believe on Him whom He hath sent,* but rather than believe, they went away and ceased the pretense of following. Is it not probable that the organized church would experience a dramatic drop in membership if every member with the same heart disposition toward Christ as had these unbelieving Jews were to cease all pretenses of following Jesus?

Men are not Christians because of what they do but because of what Christ does. Consider again the words of John 6:28,29: "What shall *we do* that *we might work* the works of God?" "*This is the work of God, that ye believe* on Him whom He hath sent" (italics mine). They were more than ready to work—even to make Christ king by force—but they were neither ready nor able to believe. And because they would not believe, nothing else they were willing to do mattered. Genuine faith is the one thing commanded and the only thing that really counts in becoming a Christian.

In seeking to clarify the crucial issue of true belief, some teachers have emphasized the difference between believing in the head and believing in the heart. This is, doubtless, an important distinction, but may I say to you there is an even greater distinction between believing in Christ and believing Christ. One can believe in Christ with both the head and the heart and never really believe Him. We have already seen an outstanding example of this. The great crowd that followed Jesus believed in Him so much they were ready to make Him king against His own will; but when He told them what to do, they ceased to follow Him.

Satan believes in Christ. The evidence makes it plain that he believes in Christ with both his head and his heart. He has no doubts concerning the central issues. He was present in much that transpired and participated directly in many of the events. He taught Judas to steal and practice deception. He aroused the Jewish leaders to crucify Christ. He helped Peter with his denials and taught the soldiers to make the false claim that the disciples had stolen the body of Jesus by night. He even put the doubt in the heart of Thomas.

The devil knows Jesus is God. He knows that Jesus died to save men from sin and self. The devil knows the power of Christ's resurrection and is convinced of the ascension of Christ to heaven. The devil even trembles at what he knows and believes. But with all his trembling, he remains obdurate still. While he believes in Christ, he will not believe Christ—that is, he will not do what Christ says.

The devil will not repent or submit himself to Christ's Lordship. The devil will not cease having his own way. Therefore, all that he believes about Jesus Christ the Lord is totally without merit and absolutely unable to help him. Satan is doomed! He has already been conquered! He will soon be cast into hell forever! Knowing all this, he still refuses to bow his knees to Jesus and submit to His Lordship. Thus he remains lost forever.

Christ made it perfectly plain to all His followers that He is Lord. He still demands yieldedness to this fact today. He insists that men cannot have two lords, for either they will hate the one and love the other or else they will hold to the one and despise the other (Matthew 6:24). Men cannot have Christ as Lord while still being lords of themselves. If Christ is to reign in a person's life, that person must cease to reign. No heart throne is large enough for two rulers. If the throne of one's life is not yielded to Christ, then that unyielded person is not believing Christ. And if he is not believing Christ, he is not a Christian. Any outward responses to Christ without genuine faith are none other than dead works which require repentance.

If you will not believe Christ on the issue of His Lordship, you cannot be saved. It does not matter what overt responses you have made toward Christ. If He is not Lord of your life, then you are lord. If you are lord you are still in your sins. Even if you can remember the exact sermon that moved you to tears and the very words of the invitation that caused you to walk down the isle, even if the face of the counselor who led you in a formula prayer is clearly remembered and the emotions of joy and relief that followed that prayer are still present and the Scripture verses of assurance provided you at that time are still remembered, if Christ is not the Lord of your life, then you have still to believe Him. Anything else you have done other than believing Him is a dead work requiring repentance and from which your conscience needs to be purged.

The great truth the coming revival must emphasize is repentance from both sins and from dead works. No dead work is more prominent in religious circles today than the formal, empty, false, legal acceptance of Christ without yielding to His Lordship in genuine faith. When a wave of God-sent repentance sweeps over the Church and false professors become genuine converts, the world will be forced to sit up and take notice.

The empty formality of accepting Christ, however, is not the only dead work being relied upon for merit with God. Church attendance and participation can be a dead work. Anyone supposing he has gained merit by attending religious services is in obvious trouble with God. Worship is always a dead work if it is not acceptable to God. Jesus told the frequently married Samaritan woman, *God is a Spirit: and they that worship Him must worship Him in spirit and in truth*

(John 4:24). God cannot be worshiped with mere human voices raised in songs of praise. Uttered prayers may not constitute worship either. If God is Spirit, how can He be worshiped by mere physical means? Men truly worship Him only when they worship Him in ways He commands. Men worship God only when they worship Him *in spirit.* It is possible to be in a physical sanctuary, singing from a hymnbook made of physical things, uttering praise with a physical tongue and listening to a sermon delivered by a physical man, while the inner spirit is miles away on the golf course or at home fussing over the Sunday dinner. If you do not worship God in spirit and in truth, all your worship is dead work. Do you need to repent of this?

Tithing and giving of offerings can be dead works. True giving is from the heart. *Every man according as he purposeth in his heart, so let him give; not grudgingly or of necessity: for God loveth a cheerful giver* (Second Corinthians 9:7). To give out of constraint or because you are embarrassed to have the offering plate pass in front of you without putting something in could hardly be described as *cheerful* giving. Some people are quick to respond to organized appeals for financial help and may give largely when their sympathies are touched, but giving done for unworthy reasons is nothing short of a dead work requiring repentance.

Any act of devotion or charity, any service rendered to others, even preaching the Word of God or teaching a Sunday school class, can be a dead work if the heart is not right before God. Have you repented of the dead prayers you have offered? Have you repented of the hymns you have sung when your heart has been empty? Have you repented of the charitable gifts you have given in the hope of recognition? Have you repented of the deeds of kindness you have shown for the praise you hoped to receive? Have you repented of all the good works you performed and expected God to notice?

We owe it to our own souls to be certain that we are not engaged in any religious actions calculated to gain merit with God or upon which we are relying to earn us mercy or favor. Surely there could be no greater tragedy than to put confidence in such erroneous thinking. The God of all mercies has made His demands plain. Let us not presumptuously suppose His Word applies to others but not to ourselves. Dead works are never acceptable to God, not even when they are ours!

Second, any work which has no capacity to be made alive by the Spirit of God is a dead work. This type of dead works may be divided into two distinct classes:

A. Those dead works which cannot be made alive by the Spirit of God because they are contrary to the mind and heart of God and erroneous in and of themselves. Consider the act of praying for the eternal salvation of those already physically dead. This is a common practice but based upon serious error. A man's eternal destiny is fixed at the time he departs this life. To pray for a change in his eternal destination after he has already died is to suppose that a second chance is provided somehow, somewhere in the afterlife. Such a supposition renders absurd the words of Hebrews 9:27,28: *And as it is appointed unto men* **once** *to die, but after this the judgment: so Christ was* **once** *offered to bear the sins of many...* (emphasis mine). Men have opportunity to repent and believe Christ in this lifetime; what they do with Christ in life determines their eternity. To pray for salvation of those already condemned because of unbelief is to ignore the plain Word of God and to engage in a work that can never be made alive by the Spirit of God.

Consider also the problem of speaking when it is time to be silent. There are occasions when words help and times when words hinder. If a person does not learn to control the tongue, he may, on occasion, speak good and sacred words without benefit to his hearers. Notice these Proverbs, *He that reproveth a scorner getteth to himself shame...* (Proverbs 9:7); *Reprove not a scorner, lest he hate thee...* (Proverbs 9:8); *A scorner heareth not rebuke* (Proverbs 13:1). From these and similar passages, it is evident that men must learn when and with whom to speak. If a professing Christian insists on sharing the Gospel at all times, in all places, and with all men, but without regard to their immediate attitudes or to the prompting of the Spirit of God, he may well be engaging in a work that will not be quickened by the Spirit and which must then be correctly labeled *dead*. Jesus Himself instructed us, *Give not that which is holy unto the dogs, neither cast ye your pearls before swine, lest they trample them under their feet, and turn again and rend you* (Matthew 7:6). To fail to heed this biblical instruction is to risk engaging in work which is contrary to the will of God and which is thus a dead work requiring repentance.

B. Those works which cannot be made alive because the worker is living in unresolved sin are even more crucial. The Psalmist was led by the Spirit of God to declare, *If I regard iniquity in my heart, the Lord will not hear me* (66:18). It is possible to pray fervently without being heard by God. Unconfessed and unforsaken sin is such a barrier between man and God that years of *praying* and *performing* religious works can be nothing but deadness. Jesus hammered this point home in Matthew 5:23,24: *If thou bring thy gift to the altar, and there rememberest that thy brother hath ought against thee; leave there thy gift before the altar, and go thy way; first be reconciled to thy brother, and then come and offer thy gift.*

Many seemingly good and useful religious works are rendered dead by unresolved sin. There are deacons who have sinned against their wives and steadfastly refuse to repent. Thus they are guilty, not only of the sin itself, but also of turning the office of deacon into a farce. There are ministers in the grip of greed whose eloquent sermons and fervent pulpit prayers are nothing but dead works. There are Sunday school teachers who minister death instead of life because their own hearts are not right with God. There are church ushers whose welcoming smiles are a mockery because they regard iniquity in their hearts. Instead of placing money in the offering plate, many a church attender needs to rise from the worship service and go out and make things right with the brother he has wronged. Is it any wonder that so many churches are more like sepulchers than healing places when those in positions of leadership are dying of the very diseases they profess to be curing in others? Why should we be surprised when unbelieving multitudes hold such churches in disdain? And if men and women outside the church are not fooled by hypocrites engaged in dead works, why should unrepentant religious workers suppose God cannot see through their thin veneer?

Please do not misunderstand me. I am not saying that the preacher who lives in unconfessed and unforsaken sin will lose his power of eloquence or pastoral abilities. I am not saying that his sermons will become dull and that he will be unable to attract crowds or that no one under his ministry will be stirred or excited, helped or blessed. To the contrary, his eloquence and power may seem greater than ever, but if his works are dead before God, does anything else matter?

The prayer of the person regarding iniquity in his heart may sound like the most fervent and sincere prayer offered during the entire Wednesday evening prayer meeting and still be dead. Unconfessed sin might not wipe the smile from the face of the usher; it might not change the pleasant disposition of the chairwoman of the missionary committee; it might not make the youth leader irresponsible and egotistical. However, if it renders their works dead, need any more be said?

When revival comes, repentance from all works which have no capacity to be made alive by the Spirit of God can be expected.

Third, any work which is done in the energy of the flesh and not in the power of the Holy Spirit is a dead work. Much preaching is dead. Many pastors cease their preparations when they know what they are going to say and have arranged it in a pleasing manner. The most difficult, and certainly the most important, part of sermon preparation is that which is done after the sermon itself is ready. If the preacher does not carefully prepare his own heart for each preaching opportunity his efforts may be nothing more than dead work. It is the Spirit, not human words, who gives life. The neglect of

earnest prayer and heart preparation is one of the gravest temptations facing the clergy today and it appears that many regularly
succumb to it.

Personal witnessing can be, indeed often is, nothing more than
dead work. It is possible to witness to another without any feelings of
love toward them, without any deep concern for their lostness and
without significant reliance upon the Holy Spirit. Indeed, some
appear to witness more for the purpose of adding up converts than
for the glory of God and the good of men. Others witness more out
of compulsion than compassion or more out of habit than heart-felt
interest in the lost and dying.

All church work—the eldership, ushering, Sunday school teaching,
choir singing, solo work, or any other of a host of good and needed
services—can be performed in the power of the flesh and not in the
power of the Spirit. In fact, it is easier and simpler to do one's
religious duty in the flesh rather than in dependence upon the Holy
Spirit. To serve in the flesh, one simply has to decide what to do and
then to do it. Perhaps most are not that crass. The general procedure
is to decide what to do, ask God in a perfunctory way to bless it, and
then proceed, presuming divine blessing.

To do everything in the Spirit is much more difficult and demanding. It necessitates searching our motives and submitting our methods
to His scrutiny. We must rely upon God to produce the results rather
than upon ourselves. For active people who like to wade into a job
and get it done and who then like to step back and admire what they
have accomplished, working in the power of the Holy Spirit can be
almost too difficult to consider.

Waiting on God is part of working in the Spirit. God's timetable
is not usually the same as man's. We want to get things done when
we are ready. Accomplishing them in the power of the Spirit will
require us to wait for God and not rush ahead of Him. Wading into
a task is usually much easier than praying hour by hour until the
Spirit of God is ready to move. But if we insist on acting ahead of the
Spirit, we should at least have the grace to admit we cherish the flesh
more than we cherish the Spirit and find no great problem with dead
works.

Have you ever wondered why revivals are so rare? It has been a
long time since a wide-scale, deep and powerful movement of the
Holy Spirit has shaken our nation. Is the God who formerly moved
His work forward so frequently by revival now operating on a
different plan? Observe these revealing words written by James
Brand, pastor of the First Church of Oberlin, Ohio, in 1883:

> *There seems to have been for the last few years an undue
> exalting of the human element in revivals, instead of laying hold*

directly of God Himself. It would seem that for some time churches have had their eyes fixed upon great movements, and have come to feel that no great results are to be expected without some mighty demonstration, and the heralding of some human evangelist. Since the time of Mr. Moody's great work in New York and Pennsylvania, revivals have declined, except in those places where these great movements have been made. This is not the fault of Mr. Moody's noble work, but the enemy is taking advantage of that work to keep the attention of Christians away from God Himself. The supernatural element has been too much ignored. People have been looking too much to externals, to methods, to men, to machinery, to "some new things," and not enough to self-abasing, heart-broken, holy prayer."[2]

Putting it bluntly, it seems easier to do the work ourselves than to wait upon God for the enduement of power from on high. Thus, much of the work conducted in the name of Jesus Christ is doomed to eternal failure because it is nothing more than dead work.

The author of Hebrews tells us that repentance from dead works is a foundational doctrine. He encourages our repentance by revealing that the blood of Jesus purges our conscience from dead works so that we might serve the living God. To be certain this repentance and this purging are accomplished is a responsibility of gigantic proportions. Are you sure it has been accomplished in you?

Have you considered the stated relationship between purging the conscience from dead works and serving the living God (Hebrews 9:14)? It is only when all reliance upon dead works has been purged from the conscience that living works can be expected. Is your trust in dead works purged? Is your pleasure in dead works gone? Do you now truly serve the living God? Revival must emphasize repentance from every known form of dead works.

REPENTANCE FROM SIN

The biblical demand for repentance, as stated earlier, is in two separate and distinct areas. Having considered repentance from dead works, we must now consider repentance from sin.

Note this critical word from Peter's second sermon (Acts 3:19): *Repent ye therefore, and be converted, that your sins may be blotted out, when the times of refreshing shall come from the presence of the Lord.* Peter did not shy from strong and plain language. His call to repentance came only after he denounced his audience for denying the holy, just One and for killing the Prince of Life (Acts 3:14,15). If

---

[2]Reverend James Brand, *Sermons from a College Pulpit.* Oberlin, Ohio, 1883, p. 43.

one doesn't know what sins he has committed he can hardly be expected to repent with thoroughness. Peter had put his finger upon the great sin of his audience. Thus, when they repented, they knew what was wrong and what sin they had to forsake.

Repentance can be of little meaning to persons who hardly perceive their sin. If a person supposes his only sin is an occasional white lie or a mildly unpleasant thought toward another person, he cannot be expected to weep bitter tears of remorse or to repent with either earnestness or permanency. A correct view of sin is mandatory if true repentance is to occur.

When King David finally felt deeply convicted of having committed adultery with Uriah's wife, Bathsheba, and of having Uriah killed, he cried to God, *Against Thee, Thee only, have I sinned, and done this evil in Thy sight: that Thou mightest be justified when Thou speakest, and be clear when Thou judgest* (Psalm 51:4). These words, when weighed carefully, are more than astonishing. David had sinned against himself. David had sinned against Israel over whom he ruled as king. David had sinned against his own family. David had sinned against Uriah. David had sinned against Bathsheba. Yet when the great error of what he had done fully broke upon his conscience with awful clarity, he saw the truly great evil of his sin as being against God.

Have you faced the fact that the great error of all sin is exactly this: it is against God. Oh, how we need to feel deeply that the greatest evil of every sin, no matter how small man may judge it, is that it is against God. Joseph, in fleeing the temptation of Potiphar's wife, was able to pinpoint the evil in the proposed act by asking, *How then can I do this great wickedness, and sin against God* (Genesis 39:9b). Do you realize the great evil of all your sin? Have you faced with trepidation the realization that it is against God that you have sinned, and in the face of His mercy committed all your evil?

Perhaps, like other deceived persons, you are satisfied that all your sins are of very minor proportion, especially when compared with David's. While you are ready to acknowledge an occasional and unimportant infraction of the law of God, do you doubt seriously that your sins are bad enough to constitute a major problem? How big does a sin have to be to be heinous? Consider these sobering words, *Whosoever shall keep the whole law, and yet offend in one point, he is guilty of all* (James 2:10). Do you realize that if you just break one tiny fraction of the law of God—one least point—your guilt before God is as great as if you broke the entire law? You may say, "I consider such a view unjust and I refuse to accept it." Such a response reveals, at best, the great deception under which you live. You have learned to accept this very principle in many insignificant areas of life. All games and sporting events have rules. How far out of bounds does a basketball player have to be before the play is voided and the basket not counted? How far off sides must the football player run before a justified penalty occurs? Many a score has been voided by a minor infraction of the rules and many a game has been lost because the least of the laws was violated. Surely, the God who made man has more right to make and enforce laws than do the designers of mere games. Face it honestly, even the tiniest infraction of God's law has earned you the permanent brand of desperately wicked *sinner*.

But are you really such a *little* sinner as you pretend? Are not your sins far more grave and more numerous than you have yet admitted? Didn't you arrive at this view of the insignificance of your sins by comparing yourself with someone else? Nearly everyone can find someone who looks worse than they do. A businessman, who faithfully supports his wife and children, can compare himself with a drunkard lying in the gutter and congratulate himself on his outstanding life of uprightness, but let that same man compare himself with the absolute standard—Jesus Christ the Lord— how will he then measure up? If the housewife, who has never actually cheated on her husband and has only occasionally considered it and not all that seriously, compares herself with the worn-out prostitute plying her trade downtown, she will look good indeed, but if she stands beside Christ, she will appear so shabby and unworthy that she will burst into tears. The drunkards and prostitutes and murderers of the world are not the standards of righteousness. God sets the standards. Jesus Christ, the incarnate God, fleshed these standards out and showed us in His own life how God expects us to live. No one has any right to compare themselves with anyone other than Christ, and no one can compare themselves with Christ and come away looking or feeling good.

We always fall short of the standard by the standard of Jesus Christ

If you insist on thinking your little sins are just against yourself and only occasionally against people, you can keep on weighing the seriousness of your sin by examining its effect upon yourself and others. A person thus deluded may ask, "If I tell this little lie, whom will it hurt?" It may appear no one will be hurt and thus a lie is justified. It is popular in our day to examine and determine the propriety of sexual relationships by asking two things: is the relationship between consenting adults? and is anyone being hurt? In the minds of many, any form of sexual conduct is acceptable if it is freely engaged in by those who are old enough to decide if they want to do it, if it is enjoyable, and if no one is greatly harmed by the act.

But suppose that instead of weighing conduct in human balances, we let the God who created sex lay down the law governing all sexual conduct. Nowhere did the Creator tell us we were at liberty to determine right or wrong on the basis of enjoyment or hurt to others.

In fact, nowhere are we told we even have the right to determine good and evil at all.

God sets the standards. God lays down the rules. The law of God is fixed and we are free neither to violate it nor to alter it. Whenever we do so, even in what may seem to us to be very minor ways, we sin against God. All sin is sin against God. All sin against God is grievously wicked and requires immediate repentance.

However, you may still not be ready to admit any serious difficulty with sin. Perhaps you believe you have never murdered or committed adultery or done any of the awful things of which so many others are guilty and therefore you have no problem. But are you being honest with yourself? Did you ever read the Sermon on the Mount? Are you aware that Jesus made the thought of sin as wicked as the act of sin. Consider His words, *Ye have heard that it was said by them of old time, Thou shalt not kill; and whosoever shall kill shall be in danger of the judgment; But I say unto you, That whosoever is angry with his brother without a cause shall be in danger of the judgment... Ye have heard that it was said by them of old time, Thou shalt not commit adultery: But I say unto you, That whosoever looketh on a woman to lust after her hath committed adultery with her already in his heart* (Matthew 5:21,22; 27,28). Do you have the gall to say you have never been angry with your brother or looked after another person with lust?

And what about all the things you should have done that you never bothered to do? Sin is not only violating the law of God in acts of commission, but in acts of omission also. When Jesus was tempted by Satan in the wilderness, He was taken to a very high mountain and shown all the kingdoms of the world and the glory of them. Satan said to Jesus, *All these things I will give Thee, if Thou wilt fall down and worship me.* Jesus responded declaring, *Get thee hence, Satan: for it is written, Thou shalt worship the Lord thy God, and Him only shalt thou serve* (Matthew 4:8-10). Can you say that you are worshiping the Lord now and that you have never served anyone but Him, not even yourself—not even for a little while? Can you, with integrity, stand before God and say the consistent pattern of your life from earliest childhood has been to worship and serve God and you have never wavered in this?

In summarizing the entire law, Jesus said, *Thou shalt love the Lord thy God with all thy heart, and with all thy soul, and with all thy mind. This is the first and great commandment. And the second is like unto it, Thou shalt love thy neighbor as thyself* (Matthew 22:37-39). Do you really love God this way? Have you ever really loved Him this much? In your present condition, can it even be hoped you ever will love God more than yourself, your own desires, or your possessions? Do you love your neighbor as yourself? Is the welfare of others always as important to you as your own welfare? Or do you justify yourself by saying you think you love your neighbor as much as your neighbor loves you. This is not the issue! If you have not even kept these two commandments which Jesus insisted were primary, how can you feel, even for a single moment, that your sins are not a serious problem?

If you are not concerned enough about your own sins to seriously face their depth and extent, what hope can you entertain for your eternal future? Do you not realize that if at any time in your entire life you have failed to love God with your entire being, you have sinned the gravest kind of sin? God has always been good to you. Year after year He has mercifully given you life and breath. Blessings upon blessings have been showered upon you. Have you demonstrated thankfulness by consistent and perfect worship? When you are accused of sin and thanklessness, who rises to your defence? The God who made you and blessed you and gave you repeated opportunities of repentance, whom you nonetheless sin against, or your own seared conscience? Do you justify yourself or does the blood of Christ justify you? Does your spirit of repentance demonstrate your gratitude or does your spirit of pride demonstrate your insensitivity?

When Peter blamed his congregation for killing the Prince of Life, he spoke fairly and justly. They crucified Christ by their unbelief. Even if their own hands did not pound the spikes into His hands and feet or thrust the sword into His side, they were responsible for these acts. But it was not only the first century Jews who crucified Christ by unbelief. Every unbelieving sinner is responsible for Christ's death. It was your very own sin that hung Christ on the cross. His precious blood was shed because of your wickedness. All the awful agony of the crucifixion of Jesus Christ was your fault. You yourself caused it. So terrible were your sins in the eyes of God that He sent His only begotten Son to suffer and die in your place. Can you view all this and still think of yourself as a little sinner scarcely needing repentance?

When the true seriousness of sin comes home to the conscience, it is not necessary to plead for repentance. The people who listened to Peter were pricked in their hearts and cried out, *Men and brethren, what shall we do?* They were told to do exactly what sinners everywhere must do, *Repent!* (Acts 2:37,38). Do you feel your sin this way? Do you care that the innocent Lord Jesus died in your place? Are you moved to compassion and shame in realizing the awful agony He suffered on your behalf? If indeed the truth of the Word of God has gripped your heart, you will not wait for any man to urge you to repent. Can you imagine a person rescued from drowning having to be forced to thank his rescuer? Can you even conceive of a person pulled from in front of a rushing train in the nick of time doing nothing whatsoever to express appreciation?

When one recognizes the awfulness of his own sin and sees Jesus as the Lamb of God who died in his place, the great question becomes: What appropriate response can I make to Him? Will a mere expression of thanks be sufficient? Can some trinket satisfy? Will a little time and a little money given to others in acts of charity suffice? Certainly not if you have faced the real facts: you were sentenced to eternal death because of the awful wickedness of your life, but Jesus died in your place. He who knew no sin became sin for you. The innocent Lamb of God took your sins upon His own shoulders and suffered for them. He gave His life for you. It was a life exchanged for a life—the life of the Son of God exchanged for the life of a miserable, hell-deserving sinner. And what response is appropriate to such a sacrifice? Is not the giving of your life to Him the only appropriate response? This is true biblical repentance.

Such repentance is not an option. Repentance from both dead works and sin is a biblical demand. Are you truly repentant? Does your repentance show? Is God Himself pleased with your repentance?

This is the great truth revival must emphasize. Without repentance, the Body of Christ is doomed to limp when it was designed to fly, to drag when it was called to draw, to drift when it should set its sails to catch every wind of the Spirit of God.

Chapter Five

What Are the Dangers of Revival?

If we look back into the history of the Church of God in past ages, we may observe that it has been a common device of the devil to overset a revival of religion; when he finds he can keep men quiet and secure no longer, then he drives them to excesses and extravagances. He holds them back as long as he can; but when he can do it no longer, then he will push them on, and, if possible, run them upon their heads. And it has been by this means chiefly that he has been successful, in several instances, to overthrow most hopeful and promising beginnings. Yea, the principal means by which the devil was successful, by degrees, to overset the grand religious revival of the world, in the Primitive Ages of Christianity, and in a manner to overthrow the Christian Church through the earth, and to make way for the great antichristian apostasy, that masterpiece of all the devil's works, was to improve the indiscrete zeal of Christians, to drive them into those three extremes of enthusiasm, superstition, and severity towards opposers; which should be enough for an everlasting warning to the Christian Church.

Though the devil will do his diligence to stir up the open enemies of religion, yet he knows what is for his interest so well, that in a time of revival of religion, his main strength shall be tried with the friends of it; and he will chiefly exert himself in his attempts to mislead them. One truly zealous person, in the time of such an event, that seems to have a great hand in the affair, and draws the eyes of many upon him, may do more (through Satan's being too subtle for him) to hinder the work, than a hundred great and strong and open opposers. In the time of the great work of Christ, His hands, with which He works, are often wounded in the house of His friends, and His work hindered chiefly by them: so that if any one inquires, as in Zechariah XIII.6, "What are those wounds in Thine hands?" He may answer, "Those with which I was wounded in the house of My friends."

The errors of the friends of the work of God, and especially of the great promoters of it, give vast advantage to enemies of such a work.

Jonathan Edwards, Northampton, Massachusetts

What Are the Dangers of Revival?

True revival can be a dangerous and exceedingly fragile blessing. Revival carries with it almost unbelievable potential for good, but the potential for evil is likewise vast. Nothing can be stronger than the unleashed spiritual power of God, bearing all before it as a mighty tidal wave. But let foolish and biblically unlearned men prevail in the days of revival and its fragility is abundantly apparent.

A brief consideration of fire and water can bring the fragility of revival into focus. Fire is one of the greatest blessings mankind enjoys. By it we warm our homes and places of employment, cook our food, heat water for our baths, purify precious metals, and shape the tools and machinery so much a part of our daily lives. Fire, under control, continually contributes to our comfort and convenience. But let that fire loose in a man's home at night while the family sleeps and tragedy will occur. Let some incendiary put a torch to a hotel and dozens of lives may be lost. Years of ardent toil can be destroyed by fire in moments, and a lifetime of savings can be turned to ashes while the fire department is racing to the scene.

Water is also a vital part of our lives. It is essential for drinking and cooking, for cleaning and growing things, and it is an abundant source of pleasure in recreations like swimming, boating and fishing. To sit beside the ocean and watch the pounding surf can be a source of relaxation and refreshment hour upon hour. But if a tidal wave comes, destruction and misery are everywhere in its path. Let the gentle rain turn to a torrential downpour and basements may flood, houses may float off their foundations, libraries may become sodden masses, machinery may cake with rust, and businesses may sink beneath acres of mud and human misery and anguish will prevail.

We cannot talk of eliminating fire and water from our lives just because they are capable of immense damage when out of control. Instead, we are constantly seeking better ways to utilize the benefits of these resources while at the same time increasing protections against their unleashed might.

In thinking of revival, we must recognize that the blessings of divine outpourings are indispensable. However, we must not fail to prayerfully and thoughtfully consider the dangers accompanying mighty movements of the Spirit of God.

Just before a great season of revival, countless Christians appear to be spiritually slumbering and the devil's work seems easy. But let revival come and the devil must get busy just to protect his existing territory. What he could accomplish before revival with ease will now take ingenuity and diligence. That the devil will not stop short while he has any hope of rendering a revival ineffectual is as certain as tomorrow's sunrise.

While no human being can predict the devil's exact strategy, certain of his methods have been used before and may be expected to appear again. When God does a great work, the devil can be counted on to produce a counterwork. As a counterfeiter, Satan has no equal. In the midst of revival we must expect to find counter-revival. While God is transforming the hearts and lives of men, the devil will be working overtime to turn things once again to his own advantage. If we fail to prepare ourselves for this inevitable counter-feit, the great revival God sends may be brought to a sudden and painful halt. What has been designed by God by way of perpetual blessing may be dissipated and largely lost.

No task preparatory to revival is more necessary or urgent than the task of learning to distinguish between the work of God on the souls of men and the counterwork of Satan. One simple observation can help: *what God does, He does for man's good; what Satan does, he does for his own good.* Consider the ramifications of this statement: God desires to pardon men's sins and give them eternal life. His work in revival is aimed at all times at man's eternal salvation. Whatever God does in the revival will bear the marks of His love and grace and will be distinguished by its direct spiritual nature and eternal value. In short, what is of God will produce a hatred of sin (including divisions among brethren); a love of prayer, the Bible, holiness, and other Christians; a compassion for those still unsaved; and an eager delight in preparing for heaven.

Satan's work, however, which is calculated for his own good without regard for the well-being of others, will focus on the temporal and the passing. We can expect him to do anything in his power to keep the eyes of men off Christ. He can accomplish this by focusing on personalities, by controversy, by physical phenomena such as prostrations, trances, and visions, or by sensational and inaccurate doctrines. If he can keep a people looking at themselves, their experiences, their feelings, and at one another, he will have assured the continued success of his own kingdom of darkness.

Time after time throughout revival history, insensitivity to the fragile nature of true revival has accounted for the sudden withdrawal of the divine presence which is always such a remarkable and essential aspect of spiritual outpourings. When God withdraws Himself because of the failure of His people to give proper biblical guidance and stability to revival, the mechanical aspects of the work may continue and even grow for a period, but in due time the counter-revival will prevail and the great work of God's kingdom will slip back to its former level.

When revival comes, a prepared people must be ready to give it guidance and direction and must be firm in preventing the work of Satan from disrupting the work of God. The preparation of such a people is, in addition to effectual, fervent prayer, of utmost importance. Such preparation requires thoughtful consideration both of Scripture and revival history. It also requires continual prayer for wisdom, spiritual discernment and courage. I emphasize courage because it will be necessary to resist Satan and his counterwork. To stand against disorders or extravagances in revival can be one of the most difficult tasks the godly will ever face. Do not be surprised if you are denounced as an unbeliever or an enemy of revival. The devil has never hesitated to stoop to such lies and he will not hesitate now. But be prepared. Give the revival guidance, resist the counterwork of Satan, and the God of revival will show Himself strong.

expect false accusations

A look at several disorders and dangers that earlier revival movements have faced can help us prepare.

DANGER ONE
Giving to Mere Human Instruments
the Glory Due to God Alone

Revival comes from God. There is nothing men can do to produce it and there is no hope of men being revived unless God revives them. God can, and sometimes does, revive His work without the use of particular human means. On most occasions, however, God has mightily used individuals in the revival of His work. To give any individual the glory due only to God is a grave error calculated to dispel the influence of the Lord and to dissipate the revival blessing. God will not share His glory with another, no matter how godly or influential that person may be. The purpose of revival is to make God, not men, famous; to focus the eyes of the people, not upon human leaders, but upon the Divine Leader; to give glory not to great men but to a great Savior.

If God chooses to revive His work through human instruments, these instruments must be regarded as chosen of the Lord for this special task. As God-ordained leaders they must be respected and honored, but not exalted. At no time should it be forgotten that they are flesh and blood like all other men. While the godly words they speak must be regarded with care and heeded with diligence, their place in God's overall plan is not more important than that of other divinely appointed leaders. To elevate revivalists above pastors, Sunday school teachers, and other faithful Christian workers is to invite confusion in the Body of Christ.

The personalities of some revival leaders may be different from those of most pastors. The methods they employ in promoting the work God has specifically called them to do must of necessity be different from those methods regularly utilized in the church. The results they see on a regular basis must differ from the results normally accompanying the work of God. But let us not err in supposing that differences in personality, methods or results entitle revival leaders to special exaltation. If the name of Jesus is magnified and the names of all human instruments are forgotten, then at least one grave danger revival faces will be eliminated.

DANGER TWO
Trying to Duplicate, by Mere Human Efforts, What Can Only Be Divinely Wrought

When revival comes, God will move it forward from place to place by His own means and on His own schedule.

People commonly have the tendency to desire what others possess. In America we sometimes call this "keeping up with the Joneses." When revival breaks out in one place, it can be expected zealous persons will desire the glorious work in their own town also. Such desire may be noble, and may well be prompted by the Holy Spirit, but it can also be very dangerous. If it drives the zealous to their prayer closets for earnest supplication and to their neighbors for confession and restitution, it is of God; otherwise, be cautious. When true revival occurs anywhere, it is manifestly God's doing. Over-anxious men, accustomed to having what they want, may not be willing to wait for God to stir mightily their own hearts and community. Such men run the risk of trying to duplicate by human efforts what a sovereign God is doing elsewhere.

People living in the midwestern and eastern portions of the United States are accustomed to hearing reports of weather moving eastward from California and the Rockies. It is frequently possible to enjoy a day or two of advance warning before a great snowstorm dumps its blanket of white upon Chicago or Boston. So too, news of revival in Colorado might well incite the people of Iowa and Nebraska to expect that the blessing of God will soon be coming their way. But expectation and preparation are certainly not the same as manipulation.

Upon hearing of the refreshing rain from heaven upon others, rush to your prayer closet and there beseech the Almighty that you may also know this divine blessing. Urge your family and friends to effectual, fervent prayer. Appoint special seasons of prayer through-out your community. Let a mighty concert of prayer demonstrate to the Father above your eager yearnings for His favor in your community. But steadfastly resist all urges to get up a revival by human efforts or means. Do not suppose that by duplicating methods used elsewhere you can also duplicate results.

Remember, Satan is eager to produce a counterwork which will run parallel with God's great work. Do not allow your zeal for having what others enjoy provoke you to accept a cheap substitute.

DANGER THREE
Focus on the Peculiar or the Sensational

We must not expect revival to proceed along ordinary lines. Being an extraordinary movement producing extraordinary results, it is sure to have some extraordinary features. Beware, however, lest the extraordinary aspects of the revival pass the bounds of biblical propriety.

The real work of revival is to quicken the Body of Jesus Christ, turning it into a vibrant, moving, spiritual force, arresting the attention of a lost world and turning the minds and hearts of countless millions to the much neglected Savior. All eyes should be focused on Him. If the focus is drawn from the Savior to some sensational feature of the awakening, there is evidence that Satan has triumphed in this instance.

Without doubt, the greatest single aspect of every true revival is the peculiar and wonderful sense of the presence of God which is manifest. It is this mighty sense of the presence of God which draws large crowds, produces intense conviction, causes tears to flow, enables hardened sinners to right the wrongs of years past, produces seemingly instantaneous conversions, and results in spontaneous joy and enthusiasm.

To focus on the crowds, the tears, the confessions, the conversions, the joy, the enthusiasm, or any other manifestation of man's reaction to the presence of Christ is unwise and deeply harmful to the true awakening. Let every eye be fixed on Jesus. He is the reviver. Men are not revived by remorse, by crowded assemblies, by magnificent preaching, or by extraordinary manifestations. Men are revived when they realize Jesus is among them. If eyes are allowed to focus on features of the revival instead of on the source, the very cause of revival will cease and the devil will have won an important round.

DANGER FOUR
Extreme Measures

In seeking to produce revival-like effects, overzealous Christian workers may be tempted to employ extreme measures which lack biblical sanction.

A natural result of true revival is a deep conviction of sin which is often accompanied by an abundance of tears and bitter remorse. It is possible, however, to have deep sorrow which is not of God. Consider Paul's word to the Corinthians: "Now I rejoice, not that ye were made sorry, but that ye sorrowed to repentance: for ye were made sorry after a godly manner...For godly sorrow worketh repentance to salvation not to be repented of: but the sorrow of the world worketh death" (Second Corinthians 7:9,10). The type of conviction and sorrow over sin that leads to true repentance must be wrought by God.

(margin note: bad example)

Some impatient workers, unfortunately, may not be content to wait for God to work. By earnest and zealous denunciation of specific sins and even of particular individuals, they may seek to produce both tears of sorrow and repentance. No preaching, however searching and sincere, is any substitute for divine power. Human effort, unaccompanied by divine influence, may frighten people and drive them to distraction, but it cannot convert.

Similarly, there is great danger in revival efforts to erect man-made standards of salvation and assurance. Beware of any professed revival leader who demands conformity to his own rules and standards. The God who made so many different kinds of men is able to convert them in as many ways as please Him. No man has the right to require another to match his experience, nor does he have the liberty to belittle another's walk with Christ because it does not parallel his own at all points.

(margin note: passion that is under control of H.S.)

While revival leaders may be expected to be men of great passion, it is also to be expected their passions will be under the control of the Holy Spirit of God. Overly severe denunciation of sin, even to momentarily depriving the elect of their comfort in Christ, can scarcely be considered passion under control. Whenever a man's zeal for the cause he espouses exceeds that of his Lord and Master, he has gone too far. Let enthusiasm be balanced with judgment; let zeal be tempered with mercy; let earnest preaching be coupled with strong prayers before the throne of the Almighty; and above all else, let the Lord of the harvest dictate the time and method of reaping. Then the revival that follows will be a source of continual joy and thanksgiving.

Dealing with extremists and preventing their excesses from disrupting the true work of God in revival are two of the most sensitive and difficult tasks you will face. Yet they are absolutely mandatory. We must not fail here.

DANGER FIVE
Neglect of Teaching and Preaching

At no time are sound biblical preaching and teaching more urgently needed in the church than during seasons of revival.

Millions of professing Christians spiritually sleep through sermons in pre-revival days. While every great truth of Scripture may have been knowingly and feelingly discussed in their presence, they may, nonetheless, be almost totally untaught in the vital doctrines of Scripture. To this host of newly revived, but largely unknowing backsliders, add the multitude of new believers flocking into the churches. It will become immediately evident that the Word of God must be set before these people with great clarity and simplicity.

Times of revival are often difficult days for teachers and preachers. Some people have the attitude: "Why should we listen to our pastor? He had nothing to say before when we slept under his ministry. Why listen to him now?" Others may find the stated services of their church insufferably dull in comparison with the revival meetings and may exasperate the pastor by their thoughtless and unwarranted comments. These reactions and others like them underline the pressing need for the systematic teaching and preaching of the Word of God, especially in times of revival. If the newly awakened are to be kept awake and if the fresh converts are to ripen into mature Christians, they absolutely must have the Word of God unfolded to them.

Continued teaching after revival.

Pastors and teachers face not only the possible resistance of the newly revived to their preaching, but also the problems of a greatly expanded ministry. Earnest men of God will find themselves hard pressed to keep up with all the demands upon their services as thousands rush into the kingdom of God. Dealing with inquirers—a task requiring precious few hours in pre-revival days—will place heavy demands upon pastors' schedules. The multiplication of public meetings and their elongated nature will fill many hours formerly spent in pulpit preparation. With both an increase in activity and an increase in the significance of what is being done, some pastors will find it very difficult to devote sufficient hours to study and sermon preparation. They may be tempted to preach less frequently and less carefully than the situation demands.

While portions of the revival meetings themselves may be given over to the sharing of experiences, it must be understood that testimonies and exhortations on the part of the recently revived backsliders and new converts cannot substitute for the orderly, Spirit-empowered preaching of the Word of God. Do not let prayer meetings or times of rejoicing, as essential and vital as they are to the revival, crowd out the Word. If every recipient of revival blessing is consistent in attendance upon the Word of God as it is faithfully preached and taught, the revival fervor will be maintained. Neglect the Word of God and no amount of excitement or fervency can turn the recently revived into the men and women of God the revival was

No substitute for preaching

calculated to produce. It is still by "the foolishness of preaching" that much of the real work of God is carried forward.

DANGER SIX
Neglect of Prayer and Private Duty
Because of the Press of Revival Activity

By their very nature, revivals tend to involve people in a flurry of fervent activity. Routines, so much a part of a normal life, give way before the extraordinary movement of the Holy Spirit. It is not uncommon for businesses, schools, and even factories to close for at least brief periods when revival is at its height. Persons of regular habits are apt to find their well-regulated lives considerably altered. Sleep, mealtimes, study periods, and hours of relaxation may yield to the demands of revival. In revival, many, who once thought it a great chore to attend church for even a single hour in a week, will now think nothing of attending protracted services daily for weeks at a time. Bible study and private prayer, once hardly thought of, will now require numerous hours weekly. With the addition of vital new demands on time, old habits and schedules must be altered.

Most disruptions of former schedules will produce far more good than harm. Men who read the daily news as if their lives depended upon it will find no great loss in curtailing that reading. Children accustomed to long hours of play each week will find better outlets for their energy. Sports-crazed youth will find the life of the Spirit more intriguing, demanding and beneficial than they ever thought possible. Businessmen will discover some of the long hours devoted to labor can be better spent in laboring for "the meat that perishes not." Even faithful housewives, who will have to sacrifice time given to meal preparation or housecleaning to the revival, will find their families all the better for the change of emphasis. When the things of the real world of the Spirit—the world of eternal certainties—crowd out the passing world of the flesh, only good can be looked for.

But there is potential danger in the great press of revival joy and blessing. Failure to maintain steady personal habits of devotion is a danger much to be feared. No amount of public praying can substitute for the prayer closet. While caught up in the thrill of seeing the Word of God grip and change the lives of those around you, beware lest you neglect your own time alone with the Bible. True prosperity of soul must always be maintained on the private level. Anyone who looks to the revival to do publicly what God Himself has ordained to be accomplished privately will find the revival as much a source of difficulty as a source of blessing. Furthermore, any family responsibilities God enjoined upon us must not suffer in the press of revival action. Maintaining a personal walk with Christ must be the goal and ambition of everyone affected by revival.

DANGER SEVEN
Unfavorable Comparisons Among Workers

Few dangers of revival are more to be feared than the human tendency to compare workers in the Lord's vineyard. Consider the current circumstances: in most churches a sizable percentage of the congregation seems to be spiritually asleep. They may attend church services with regularity and yet be unsound in the faith and without deep concern for the welfare of their souls. While in some instances the pastor may be less fervent than the glory of God demands, in most cases the problem lies squarely with the slumbering parishioners. If true revival comes to these churches and the sleeping multitudes are awakened to vital godliness, their immediate tendency will be to blame the pastors for all the good things they missed during the years in which they took their souls' ease.

If a human instrument from outside their church is involved in their awakening, they will be strongly tempted to compare this instrument with their pastor. No matter how earnestly he may have sought their spiritual good in days past, some of these newly awakened face the danger of harshly judging the man of God who long looked after their souls. Even if the newly awakened have strong reason to suppose their pastor did not care sufficiently for their spiritual welfare, what right do they now have to censure him? If they themselves were asleep, who are they to belittle their pastor if he was sleepy also?

Instead of comparing one leader with another, let all the newly revived learn to pray for all who minister the Word of God. Let the God of all men, ministers included, deal as He pleases with His own instruments.

An equally dangerous tendency is comparing the preaching style and the ability of one man with another. It ought not to surprise anyone that men who itinerate in revival work are often more persuasive and fluent in the pulpit than some pastors. Generally speaking, they have far more practice, speak on fewer themes, are frequently repeating the very same material, and so ought to excel in their own special calling. Any temptation to make comparisons must be steadfastly resisted. Be content to know the sovereign God uses men and gifts as it pleases Him. Let God be God! Keep your eyes on Him, not on His workers!

DANGER EIGHT
The Exaltation of Novices

A common tendency in revival movements has been to give position

and place to new converts that they do not have the grace or
Christian stature to handle. There is something very refreshing about
hearing the testimony of a person newly turned to Christ. Who could
forbid this? Who would wish to stop the mouths of babes? But is
there godly wisdom in exalting persons above their divinely ordained
places? The Scriptures plainly teach that the place of the new convert
is not a position of leadership among established Christians (First
Timothy 3:6).

During the Welsh revival [1904-05] many of the new converts
were rushed from place to place to give their witness and to exhort
others to share their experience. Unfortunately it became common
for these "babes in Christ" to speak abusively of aged saints who did
not share their precise revival experience. Having had no opportunity
to mature in their Christian experience, they had no basis for even
comparing immaturity with spiritual depth. Some of these young
converts, largely untaught in the ways of Christ, resorted to tactics
wonderfully used by Satan to bring the revival to an early end.

New converts and the freshly revived both need time to put down
spiritual roots—learning to pray and to study the Word of God,
gaining mastery over the flesh, and maturing into lasting vessels of
divine grace. If thrust to the forefront of revival activity too early in
their Christian pilgrimage, they may fail to realize their own need of
growth and development. If the novice is not carefully nurtured by the
church, his own pride may rush to the fore, and he who should have
become a giant in the Lord may turn into an arrogant, hypocritical,
spiritual runt.

While nothing must be done to hinder the usefulness of revival
converts, everything humanly possible must be accomplished to see
that they grow and develop into the likeness of Jesus Christ. Any
undue exaltation will seriously hamper their personal growth and will,
in time, disrupt the work of the Spirit of God.

DANGER NINE
Encouraging Party Spirit

Revival movements throughout history have been plagued by conflict.
In American revivals we have seen the Old School versus the New
School; the Old Measures pitted against the New Measures; the Old
Lights fighting the New Lights. Long ago Satan discovered that if he
could get Christians fighting among themselves over the revival, his
hard work would be nearly over.

Every effort must be made to keep the revival free of party spirit,
but I plead with you to remember that all the seeds of conflict are
already in the soil. No fresh discord needs to be invented. All the
devil needs to do is to encourage professing Christians to keep on

doing what they do so very well, and the lovely fruit of revival will turn to a spoiled and putrid mess.

If revival is to prevail, if revival blessings are to spread, if the precious name of Jesus is to be exalted throughout the whole earth, then Christians must commit themselves to being different. All nonessential controversial issues must be set aside. Does it really matter which denomination prospers most if the kingdom of God is surging forward in power? What possible difference can it make if a particular interpretation of a secondary doctrinal issue prevails or loses ground if the hearts of men and women everywhere are truly turning toward Jesus Christ in repentance and saving faith? How can methods of church work matter when the Founder and Head of the Church is manifesting Himself among His people in an unusual and wonderfully reviving way?

The crucial word in what I have just said is obviously *nonessential*. Perhaps every schismatic in history was certain he split the Body of Christ over essentials, but in the Judgment, when full light shines, the facts will declare otherwise. The revival God is going to send must not be destroyed by infighting. See that you are not a tool of the devil in tearing down what God is building.

DANGER TEN
Censoriousness

Revival does not touch all persons equally. Some need revival far worse than others. Some, already revived, are the human instruments God uses in advancing revival. Others, by their very natures and by their understanding of spiritual things, will perceive revival in an essentially different light from us. We must not allow ourselves the foolish luxury of supposing that all true children of God will regard the movement of the Holy Spirit in the same exact light and will be equally affected by it. From such erroneous thinking comes the grave danger of a censorious spirit.

The newly revived and hopefully converted must especially beware of the danger of thinking or speaking ill of those who have not experienced the revival in the same way they have. If you are a new convert, remember it is not your place to rebuke aged Christians. Try not to forget that while you luxuriated in your sins, faithful Christians were praying for you. While you wasted your life in riotous living, these Christians moved the Kingdom of God forward by their tears and sacrifices. Do not be surprised that they have not felt what you have felt in the revival and cannot describe an experience which is precious and valuable by your standards. Furthermore, do not think ill of them when they make it plain they are not yet ready to turn the work over to you. If they regard you as immature, seek their help in growing up in Christ. God has called both of you into the kingdom for such a time as this. If each one will occupy his rightful place before God, the revival can move on in wave after fresh wave of blessing. However, if Christians begin to censure one another, the Spirit of God will be grieved.

So also, aged Christians must beware lest they think or speak ill of the fire and enthusiasm of the newly revived. If you are tempted to belittle their experience with God or to suggest they might still fall backward into their old ways, rush to your prayer closet and there beseech God to give you a caring heart so that you may nurture and encourage these lambs of the flock.

All Christians alike must beware of thinking and speaking ill of divinely ordained servants of Jesus Christ. Not every pastor is able to enter into revival work with the same joy and openness. Those who stand aloof are not designed by God to be targets of your abuse. Pray for them if you will, but do not speak ill of any of God's servants. Every man answers to his own Master. Do not lose sight of this Gospel fact!

DANGER ELEVEN
Pride and Jealousy

While these twin sins are doubtless always present with us, their capability of doing harm, when exercised in the midst of revival, cannot be overstated.

It is no easy thing for a pastor who has ministered to a congregation for years to hear large numbers of his regular members acknowledging they have just found Christ during the revival. It takes a lot of grace for such a pastor to rejoice with his people and not to resent in any way the revival leader instrumental under God in their experience. This is especially true if the pastor baptized these people himself and received them into the fellowship of his church, all along supposing, with them, that they were genuinely converted.

Nor is it easy for a man who has preached his heart out for years to a small handful of seemingly indifferent people to see vast crowds gather in his own church to listen to an itinerant revival leader who perhaps lacks polish and education and whose strongest point seems to be a mysterious sense of God in all he is and does.

It is even to be expected that some new converts, still lacking many of the graces of Jesus, will belittle a pastor's work to his face and make it plain they find his preaching "dry stuff" in comparison with what they have feasted upon in the midst of revival.

All true servants of Jesus must prepare their hearts for such onslaughts. Let every man of God determine now that no personal pride or feelings of jealousy will in any way hinder the work of Christ in revival. If a minister of Christ cannot stand this kind of abuse, if he cannot rejoice in true conversions even from among his own flock, if he cannot accept with gladness of heart his place in the kingdom of God, he has every reason to cry to God day and night for deliverance:

> Oh, to be saved from myself, dear Lord,
>   Oh, to be lost in Thee.
> Oh, that it may be no more I
>   But Christ who lives in me.

While one pastor is vexed with jealousy, another may be tempted to pride. Some pastors will receive more converts into their churches than others. Some men who formerly had seemingly little impact will be mightily used of God in revival work. Christian workers have no right to look to themselves or their situations. Let the God of revival dictate whom He will exalt and whom He will humble. If every eye is upon Him and upon what He is doing, the blessed work will move forward. Pride and jealousy must perish so that the name of Jesus may be exalted.

DANGER TWELVE
Exaggeration Or Distortion of the Truth

If we could suppose the devil would take a long nap as soon as revival begins, this warning might not be necessary. But, knowing as we do the increased fervency of his efforts in seasons of revival, we need to look squarely at this critical danger.

Some men who labor in evangelistic and revival-type work are known as distorters of the truth. The practice of exaggerating statistics has been so common that the expression "evangelistically speaking" has been coined to describe this evil. If a thousand are present in a meeting, we may later read of the vast crowd of thousands who thronged the auditorium. If ninety-seven came forward in response to the altar call, a few of them to seek the Lord, and some of them for rededication, and an undetermined number to see the evangelist close up, we may later be surprised to hear that more than one-hundred were converted in that meeting. Such exaggerations may be accepted in some circles, but they are not certainly acceptable with the Lord. The God who sends revival is the God of truth. No false accounting is acceptable to Him, and all such fabrication of truth can be guaranteed to disrupt the work of God in revival.

Revival is not built upon men's reputations of success as soul winners or as those who reclaim backsliders. No reporting of statistics, true or false, is essential to the real work of the Holy Spirit of God who keeps His own records of what He is doing. God does not need the help of human statisticians, much less dishonest ones.

There is not only the temptation to exaggerate statistics, but also the danger of stating as facts things which cannot be known for certain. It is unwise not only to declare the number of converts as the result of any given work, but also to declare any individual as a convert. Let the spirit of God reveal the converts. We must learn to hedge our pronouncements with such expressions as "hopefully converted" or "apparent subjects of awakening" as our godly fathers did.

DANGER THIRTEEN
The Media

Revival is news; religion generally is not. When true revival comes, the media are certain to be interested. A current sense of duty may occasionally prompt them to cover certain religious conventions and events which even insiders consider a bore. In order to provide a bit of spice and interest, media people may tend to focus on the controversial or the unusual. When revival comes, the media will not need to be begged to attend. They will, however, need to be urged to speak the truth, the whole truth, and nothing but the truth.

True lovers of revival understand that the media report what they can *see*. Of necessity, they must focus on the visible. Because the real work of revival is invisible, the media coverage is apt to lack balance and perspective. Knowing this, we may anticipate a media focus on the extreme and the bizarre to the frequent neglect of the deeper and more vital, but less visible, aspects of the awakening. Because reporters cannot interview the Author of revival, they will have to make do with the recipients of revival blessing. Consequently, we must expect media reports of revival to be long on experience and short on divine perspective.

Wherein lies the danger? It lies in fixing attention upon the visible and passing effects of revival instead of upon the Lord of revival Himself. Revival news usually stirs revival-like activity. We can then expect undisciplined religious persons to seek to duplicate the effects of the revival the media have portrayed without seeking the face of the invisible God who has sent the awakening.

Even in welcoming candid reporting by honest media representatives, every lover of revival needs to be aware of the grave danger extensive publicity poses. Any over concentration on the readily observable and easily reproduced physical phenomena of a spiritual movement is to be viewed with great caution.

Revival is good news but counter-revival is bad news. The devil is more dependent upon publicity for the advancement of his work than God is. Focus on the bizarre and sensational is bound to do more for the kingdom of darkness than for the kingdom of light, especially in our age of instantaneous worldwide telecommunication.

When revival news focuses on God and His glory, every believer has reason to rejoice. Any other focus is cause for great concern.

DANGER FOURTEEN
Scandalous Confessions

The public confession of sin is a regular and necessary aspect of true revival, but failure to regulate public confession invites reproach and shame upon the movement, as well as the downfall of weak souls. At all times there needs to be careful adherence to the following guidelines for confession.

Those who have sinned privately need to make private confession. To make public confession of private sins is not only unnecessary but terribly dangerous. Consider the common problem of lust. Lust is a private sin. If a man stands before a public assembly and confesses his lust for women, as some have done by naming specific women who have been the objects of their lustful thoughts, far greater evil will be stirred up than put down. Every person about to make public confession should ask, "Is my sin known by this assembly? Has it affected them? Will my confession of it aid or hinder the work of God in my soul and theirs?" If the honest answers to this self-examination are negative, no public confession should be made.

Those who have sinned against individuals need to approach those individuals, confess their sins, and make things right. If the position you now hold was obtained by knocking another person down and standing on him, you need to go to that person and make it right. If you have stolen from or defrauded any individual, you need to confess your sin to that individual. However, if your sin against an individual is generally known by his family and has affected their lives and their view of you, then confession to this larger group is in order. In short the circle of confession should be as broad as the circle of the sin's influence. Do not seek some cheap and easy way in making confession. If you have sinned grievously against a person and badly damaged them by your sin do not think that a quick telephone call is a satisfactory method of making the wrong right. Whenever humanly possible, make your confession face to face with the person or persons damaged by your sin.

Some sins are certainly against a much larger audience than an individual or a family and can only be truly confessed publicly. Consider the case of a church member who starts a vicious rumor against his pastor. Lies and rumors seldom remain private and must therefore be confessed to all who hear them directly or indirectly. The originator of the lie or rumor ought to confess his sin, and every person who helped spread it has reason to confess his sin also. If a church treasurer has stolen funds from the congregation, he must make public confession and restitution. If a pastor or an elder has neglected to pray for his flock and to care for their souls as he vowed he would when placed in that high and holy office, he needs to confess his sins of failure to that very congregation. Sunday school teachers who have taught trivia instead of the great truths of God need to confess this sin to the class. Politicians who have defrauded the people who elected them to office must make public confession and restitution to their entire constituency. Every sin against the public needs to be confessed to the specific group which has been sinned against.

Two grave dangers threaten all confession: *too little and too much.* Beware lest your concern for propriety and pride keep you from confessing those sins your public deserves to hear about. Likewise, beware that your earnestness in making all things right before God does not play into the hands of the great deceiver who would love to turn your confession of sin into an inducement for another's ruin.

DANGER FIFTEEN
Lack of Discernment

It must not be supposed, for even a single moment, that all that occurs in the name of revival is automatically of God. At no time in its history is the Church more subject to error than in the midst of revival blessing. One of the gravest dangers facing revival is the failure of revival leaders and subjects to discern between the work of God on the souls of men and the work of the devil on their bodies in the counter-revival. Scripture teaches the urgent necessity of "trying the spirits." Let everything that is done in revival come under the careful scrutiny of the written Word of God.

In certain past revivals, physical manifestations have been supposed to indicate the presence and work of the Holy Spirit. Falling into trances and being taken with the jerks are among those phenomena highly regarded by some lovers of revival. Do the Scriptures indicate a fixed relationship between the physical and the spiritual? The evidence plainly proves that a person can experience such physical phenomena without any permanent spiritual good being accomplished. Even such a highly desirable physical manifestation as tears of conviction does not of necessity demonstrate a saving work accomplished by Christ in the soul. I remind you again, when God does a great work, Satan can be expected to produce a counterwork. God works primarily in the soul; the devil works primarily on the body. Any encouragement, or even toleration, of extreme physical phenomena runs the constant risk of drawing the minds and hearts of people away from the holiness of God and their urgent need of repentance.

Everything that occurs in revival should be tested: Is it in accord with the Word? Does it distract from the spiritual work which God is doing? Does it result in permanent spiritual improvement? Does it give glory to God? Will it advance the revival or hinder it? The focus must be kept on God. To give place to the devil in these matters, even for a few moments, is an evil too great to consider.

Remember the Church has been on this planet nearly 2000 years and there is a lot of history to study. In the Evangelical Revival in England in the eighteenth century, physical phenomena such as swooning were originally accepted and even encouraged in the public meetings. In time, George Whitefield, Charles Wesley, and others prohibited trances, swoons, and similar occurrences in their services. As a result of this courageous stand against the counter-revival, the movement of the Holy Spirit remained alive and well for a prolonged and blessed time. In America, Jonathan Edwards and his associates likewise put down all types of sensationalism and extremism and by their discerning oversight were able to extinguish many of the brush fires of wild enthusiasm which would have destroyed the real work of God.

Whenever there is spiritual focus on the physical, grievous dangers lurk. Discerning saints must learn the true test of the manifest presence of God. Contrary to popular thinking it is not demonstrations of power or displays of joy and excitement. The devil is perfectly capable of splendid appearing frauds in these realms. There is one realm, however, where the devil has no capacity and no desire to counterfeit and that is in the realm of holiness. Biblically, whenever the manifest presence of God was experienced by men it was accompanied by a terrible sense of the awfulness of sin and some overt expression of this terror such as crying out, "Woe is me, I am undone" or "Depart from me, for I am a wicked man." If holiness is not the immediate and lasting outcome of any supposed experience, it is automatically suspect.

I urge you to determine here and now to learn to discern the true work of God and to keep it free from the counterwork of Satan. Other godly people will join you in this labor. Although you may be jeered and mocked by well-meaning but deluded persons, be assured that the God of revival will honor your efforts to keep His name and work pure.

DANGER SIXTEEN
Neglect of the Whole Counsel of God

The very nature of revival makes emphasis on certain essential truths mandatory. A sleeping church will specialize in comforting and soothing truths, usually to the neglect of the alarming and arresting portions of Scripture. Revival leaders must guard against making the same error but in the opposite direction. Let it be clearly stated, *A revival out of balance is soon a revival out of power.*

The whole Word of God is the correct message of revival. While certain key words and expressions will unquestionably come to the fore, the revived church cannot afford to neglect any portion of the Scripture and must mold and shape its ministry and growth accordingly. If revival is to be sustained, systematic preaching and teaching of the entire Word of God is mandatory. In earlier generations, revival converts might have had a considerable background of biblical truth and morality upon which to immediately draw, but most of today's hopeful converts will have very little, if any, knowledge of the Bible. Therefore the urgent necessity of balanced biblical teaching and preaching can hardly be overemphasized.

Revival converts and reclaimed backsliders will never become sturdy Christians if fed a pablum diet of alarmist eschatology and rudimentary salvation truths. The grounds of biblical morality must be laid upon them quickly or they may be lured back into the ways of the world. If the holiness of God, His sovereignty over all the earth, His hatred of sin, and His just retribution of sinners are not declared in all their power, the revived will soon be so confused by the world that they will have neither the strength nor the equipment to stand against the wiles of the devil. The entire Word of God is not only suitable for doctrine and instruction in righteousness, but also necessary for proper growth and development in the life of the Spirit.

Let revival leaders beware of both overstating and understating the truths of the Bible. While the severe warnings and denunciations of the Prophet are badly needed in this hour, so are the life-giving truths of the Epistles. While men need to see and feel the love of God so beautifully shown in the death, burial, and resurrection of Jesus Christ, they also need to realize that it is a fearful thing to fall into the hands of the living God. Let the whole counsel of God prevail in revival, and the blessed work of God will go on from strength to strength.

What will be the consequence of failing to consider seriously the dangers outlined above? It will be to invite the early end of a badly needed and fervently sought revival. The greatest single object in revival must always be the glory of God. This glory of God must be protected and preserved by men. With earnest prayer, careful heart-searching, and courageous and discerning action, men and women of God can protect the glorious reviving work of God against loss and corruption. It is a matter of caring! Do you care enough to prepare yourself for this great work? Do you care enough to stand against the counterwork when it appears? Do you care enough to see the glory of God upheld at any personal cost?

Chapter Six

What
Hinders
Revival?

The last thing to which I would call your attention, as a hindrance to a revived state of religion, is the want of a right state of mind among real Christians in regard to such a revival. In what do we conceive such a state of mind properly to consist? Chiefly in two things—Faith in the possibility of the work, and a sense of personal responsibility in regard to its production.

1. Faith in its possibility—faith, that is, to believe that it is not a vain and chimerical thing—a fine or extravagant idea floating in the brain of a heated enthusiast—but a state of things which, as it often has been, so may it again be realized and seen amongst men...

2. This however, is not all; for with faith in the possibility of a revival, there must be a sense of personal responsibility in regard to the means necessary for producing it. That it is God's work, requiring at every step the interposition of His hand, and manifesting often in a singular manner the sovereignty of His grace, does not the less render it dependent upon the instrumentality of His people; and if the greatness of the effect appears many times so completely out of proportion to the smallness of the means employed, that we feel constrained to look almost exclusively to the hand of God, so far from regarding this as proof that little or no account should be made of human instrumentality, it should but stimulate us the more diligently to employ it, as being evidently crowned by God with such superabundant honor and blessing. But to put forth the instrumentality necessary to bring about, or to sustain such a revived state of religion, a feeling of personal responsibility on the part both of pastors and people, is indispensable. In the pastors no doubt first and most prominently—but not in them alone— there must be the sympathy of other hearts, leading to the united cooperation of other hands. But if men sink the feeling of their own responsibility, in that of the minister of the church at large—if, seeing so much iniquity prevailing and so many difficulties standing in the way of reformation, they look each one to his neighbor for giving the requisite application, and satisfy themselves with the thought that they can do little or nothing in the matter, what reasonable expectation can be entertained of the needed reformation ever taking place? Who then will pray as if any thing depended on the success of his prayers? Who will manifest a proper and becoming concern for the prevailing sinfulness? Who will order his conversation, and lay out his talents and use his opportunities, as if it stood with him in a measure to turn the tide of ungodliness and revive the interests of piety... Oh! that we could get you to feel aright the obligation which rests on you as individuals to promote this divine work—we should not despair of vanquishing every other difficulty and dislodging every other hindrance.

Patrick Fairbairn, Bridgeton, Scotland

What Hinders Revival?

It has been a long time since America and the English-speaking world have been visibly shaken by the power of the Spirit of God. Why must most of us acknowledge we have never been part of a deep and powerful revival? Is it because the Lord has ceased to send revivals? Has He found a better way to promote His work than by periodic awakenings? Or are there severe hindrances to true revival built into the very structure of our lives, our churches, and our society?

Those who pretend no serious interest in revival can scarcely be expected to deeply concern themselves with these questions. But what about the rest of us who profess a great concern for the things of God and a belief in revival? Could we ourselves be the major reason revival does not come? Are we the hindrances? We owe it to God, to ourselves, and to our children, to searchingly analyze this possibility and face the results with integrity.

PASTORAL HINDRANCES TO REVIVAL

A necessary place to begin is with pastors. The role of the pastor affects virtually all aspects of Christian endeavor. His influence for good or evil is truly profound. The depth of the pastor's responsibility for the revival of the work of God in his own parish is staggering. To be an instrument that God can mightily use in revival should be the earnest desire of every divinely appointed leader of a spiritual flock. Failure to give godly leadership in seeking times of unusual spiritual awakening could be the most serious flaw in any pastor's entire ministry. Opposing the work of God in any way and hindering the progress of those crowding into the kingdom during days of revival harvest are terrible sins against God and His people.

Pastor, have you considered the Epistle of Jude with great care? This small letter is much more than a homilist's gold mine. It is an immensely sensitive portrayal of the breakdown of Christian leadership within a local church. Without trying to give a thorough exposition of this searching word from God, let me draw your attention to the opening denunciation of unworthy leadership: *For there are certain men crept in unawares, who were before of old ordained to this condemnation, ungodly men, turning the grace of our God into lasciviousness and denying the only Lord God and our Lord*

Jesus Christ (verse 4). A large portion of the remainder of the epistle is an expansion of this indictment against leaders in the church who occupy positions which they have gained unworthily—by stealth and deception.

After exposing the wickedness by several series of illustrative views which appear in combinations of three, Jude breaks his symmetrical pattern by utilizing five natural similitudes of promise (verses 12-13) which clearly reveal the emptiness of the ministry of these impostors. Through these images, Jude reveals the tragedy of all leaders who give great promise of good, but who are, instead, sore disappointments to their congregations. Consider first the promises these similitudes seem to offer:

1. Reefs (spots), indicating natural harbors in which ships may safely winter and which shelter the shoreline from fierce storms.

2. Clouds, suggesting the promise of rain so crucial to sustaining life and producing fruit.

3. Trees, shielding from the burning rays of the sun and bearing fruits of delight and nourishment.

4. Waves, speaking of constancy, certainty, and for the weary and perplexed, a wonderful source of relaxation in watching them beat upon the shore.

5. Stars, guiding men's ships for generations and crucial in many of our scientific calculations, even today.

Now notice the emphasis Jude makes in his utilization of these similitudes.

1. Reefs. Instead of providing safe harbor for the ship of grace, these supposed Christian leaders are so self-centered they feed themselves at the agape feast without regard to the welfare of others. In consequence, instead of providing safety and certainty for the church and its people, they are like uncharted reefs upon which ships are dashed and destroyed.

2. Clouds. Instead of bringing promised rain to refresh the spiritually parched people of God, these men are like clouds without water, carried about by the winds.

3. Trees. Instead of providing luxuriant green leaves and plentiful, succulent fruit for the benefit and blessing of the church, these pretenders are like trees without fruit, twice dead, plucked up by the roots.

4. Waves. Instead of providing the steady, encouraging, strength-renewing benefits that a trip to the ocean-shore can produce, these pastors rile the congregation as raging waves of the sea and in the process are foaming out their own shame.

5. Stars. Instead of providing that absolutely reliable guidance and direction by which the people of God can chart their lives, these false prophets are like wandering stars for whom is reserved the blackness of darkness forever.

And what of the congregation that sits under the ministry of such men? The people may come with hungry hearts, hoping to hear a clear word from God. They may assemble eagerly and expectantly, only to be grieved and disappointed time after time. Those who were appointed to feed them the truth of the Word of God feed themselves upon wickedness. Those who were paid to refresh the souls of others in the things of the Spirit, steal the blessing from their people. Rather than providing nourishment for the soul, they cause the people to wither yet more and more. Commissioned to convey spiritual graces, these leaders are, in fact, themselves graceless. Those who were to be pillars of strength and guides to the wanderers are the very curse they promised to overcome.

Every pastor who presides over a flock of God must searchingly inquire if his ministry is in any way a disappointment to his people. Shouldn't every true servant of Jesus Christ discern whether he gives more promise in his ministry than he fulfills? Pastor, is there any danger you might be depriving your people of revival blessing? Is it possible that instead of being an instrument of great good, you have become a blockade beyond which the extraordinary graces of the Spirit of God in revival cannot flow?

Your people have every right to expect profound and powerful spiritual blessings from your ministry. They have reason to look to you as a shining light, a pillar of strength, a tree of righteousness, a harbor of divine graces, a harbinger of showers of blessing. The question is, *are they or will they be disappointed?*

Are you willing and able to fulfill the rightful spiritual expectations of your people? Do the hungering and thirsting correctly look to you? Are the weary and heavy-laden gladdened at your doorstep? Does your congregation thrill and rejoice in the spiritual feast you set before them each Lord's day? Do your people rightly regard you as a giant of the faith after whom they can pattern their lives? Can your people look to you knowing they will not be disappointed? And especially, as the Spirit of God waters the earth afresh with revival blessings, are your parish and your personal ministry among the recipients of these heavenly showers? Is your holy and consecrated life at the forefront of those giving blessing to the fainting multitudes?

In giving the thoughtful consideration these inquiries deserve, a pastor must take these matters before the Lord in earnest prayer. Some years ago it was reported that an American evangelist visited Scotland and personally denounced prominent clergymen by name. Several of them banded together in a move to force the evangelist out of the country, but one of their number fled to his study and there on his face before God cried out, "What a wicked man I am that even a foreigner is offended by my sins!" Need we ask which of these men found favor with God?

In 1832, Ebenezer Porter wrote a series of letters to the Revival Association at Andover Theological Seminary in Massachusetts in which he gave something of the history of American revival movements during the early part of his century and some very practical advice and help to the seminary students. In the third of these letters, Porter kindly described hindrances to revival in *four brief pastoral portrayals* of good men who could not be charged with any heresy, immorality, or particular hostility to revivals, but who could not expect to see revival in their churches, even when revival blessings were found in churches all around them:

Portrait One:

A—— was one of those good men who were under the dominion of a sluggish temperament. To him the maxim, "Expect great things, attempt great things," however proper in secular enterprises, seemed little short of presumption, as applied to the ministry. Effort, beyond the most obvious claims of official duty, he dreaded. To travel from one side of his parish to another, especially to travel half way across a county, to attend a meeting of ministers or churches, cost him as much self-denial as it cost Caesar to cross the Alps and subdue a kingdom. In fulfilling his pastoral appointments, he was always behind the time, he always made on his hearers the impression of languor and inefficiency in his movements, and imparted to them too much of his own spirit. No revival, or none of much power and extent, was witnessed in his congregation.

Portrait Two:

B—— was a man of literary taste, an idolater of books. He was so fond of reading, especially works of genius and popular literature, that the spirituality of his heart was gradually impaired; he laid down his favorite authors with reluctance, to attend a prayer meeting; went to fulfill an engagement, with little of pastoral feeling; and returning to his study, became absorbed in his intellectual pursuits, instead of his appropriate work, as one appointed to "watch for souls." Rare instances of conversion, but no revival occurred under his ministry.

Portrait Three:

C—— was fond of social avocations. Lively in temper, he easily persuaded himself that both his health and usefulness would be promoted by association with cheerful company, and by mingling, at times, in fashionable visits and scenes of amusement. On these occasions, deeming it proper to show the opposers of religion that it requires no austerity of manners, and that a Christian minister need not always maintain the aspect of gravity, he often passed to the other extreme of levity, and even frivolity, in conversation. Though he was an able, and sometimes a powerful, preacher, and irreproachable in general morals, the habit of jesting and story-telling, which he had insensibly acquired, destroyed the savor of godliness in his pastoral intercourse, and exerted a deadly influence on his ministry. His witty anecdotes more than counteracted the good tendency of his sermons. He saw no revival among his people.

Portrait Four:

D—— impaired his pastoral usefulness by the voluntary multiplicity of his secular cares. He was not merely provident and frugal in all his domestic arrangements, as Christian duty requires every minister to be, but he gradually acquired a passion for gain. This led him to engage in transactions incompatible with the absolute consecration which he had made of himself in his holy calling. If he did not descend to any of those sordid expedients denominated by the Apostles [as the] love of "filthy lucre," he became proverbially an adept in bargains and business, till these engrossed his time, and rendered him in spirit a secular man. When a revival which prevailed around him seemed to have begun among his own congregation, it soon ceased, because the pastor could not find time to help it forward.[1]

Our century has added another four portraits which require the same prayerful self-scrutiny.

Portrait Five:

E—— was in the grip of unresolved personal problems. For years there existed serious tension in his home and his relationship with his wife was on a continually deteriorating basis. While there were occasional weeks when the home was not torn by verbal strife, it was not uncommon for him to appear in the pulpit immediately following one of these frequent arguments. Both Pastor and Mrs. E—— made every effort to hide the tensions from the congregation, but several of the perceptive and loving members of his parish were aware of the ongoing hostilities. While diligent in the preparation of his sermons, and as faithful as his situation permitted in carrying out his pastoral duties, there was a marked hesitancy in his preaching and a general ineffectiveness in his total ministry. Several other churches in his neighborhood enjoyed powerful stirrings of revival, but his church continued in its gradual decline.

Portrait Six:

F—— was a lover of words. It was impossible for him to imagine any calling or profession more delightful and honorable than the

---

[1]Ebenezer Porter. *Letters on the Religious Revival which Prevailed about the Beginning of the Present Century.* Boston, 1858, p.36ff.

pastorate. Preaching was sheer delight. So eloquent and moving did he find his own words, he could scarcely understand the restrained manner in which people congratulated him upon his preaching. He was able to find the most obscure texts of Scripture and adorn them with such a breadth of beauty and fascination that it seemed the whole world would in time be in attendance at his services. Vast crowds hung upon his every word. When the sanctuary overflowed, a second and then a third morning service were added, and still the people came in ever-increasing numbers. When a hugh new auditorium was built, it soon filled to overflowing. His preaching was essentially biblical and his personal life was a happy example of many sterling qualities, but when revival shook his city, his own church scarcely felt the slightest stirring. Worse still, the revival was not missed. Contentment in the kingdom of words kept his church from the kingdom of power.

Portrait Seven:

G——— was an arresting Gospel preacher. His fervent pulpit appeals seemed to convey the greatest possible passion for souls. He could be expected to be at the forefront of every evangelical endeavor. None of his many acquaintances in the ministry seemed to stand even shoulder high to this towering giant of inflamed zeal and vitality. However, he lacked moral earnestness. While he was a giant in the eyes of men, he was a midget before God. His prayer life had the vitality of a dead hedge. His application of Scriptural truth to his own life was only well accomplished publicly. His own children understood him well and did not attend his ministry. In the early years of their marriage, his wife was disappointed by the contradictions in his spiritual life, but it was easier to join him in duplicity than continually to urge the practice of the presence of God. They were a striking couple and got along beautifully, but the God who knew them well withheld revival blessing from their lives and ministries.

Portrait Eight:

H——— seemed to be the embodiment of all the best characteristics of a much loved and useful pastor. He was always tender in his dealings with his people. A parishioner could scarcely face the smallest problem without this dear man being there with a word of encouragement and help. The children all loved him for remembering their names and speaking kindly to them in private. The aged blessed God upon every remembrance of his gracious solicitations after their physical welfare. People of all ages enjoyed his thoughtful sermons, well-planned services, and gracious personal approach. The pulpit committee that had sought him out and recommended him to the congregation were often thanked for the excellent service they had performed in securing this good man. Year after year he continued faithfully to serve his people and they were glad. But no revival ever touched his work. From his earliest days in the seminary, he was uncertain of the doctrines that others considered essential. While he never willfully plagued people with his own doubts, they were always there. Although his secret doubts were largely unknown to his congregation, it was only those who listened for what he did not say that perceived his problem. The fruits of his uncertainty were manifested in his own lack of spiritual depth and power and in the unconverted condition of a large portion of his congregation.

Is it possible that you fit one or more of these pastoral portraits? Does prayerful self-scrutiny reveal all is well, or do you find yourself in need of heartfelt repentance and God-sent revival? If at this time God were to give His people pastors according to His own heart, would you be His gift to them or would you be set aside?

Throughout history pastors have either been great friends or great foes of revival. For a pastor, a genuine revival can be either a source of marvelous joy or a cause of great upset and anguish. Some pastors would welcome at any time the evidence of an extraordinary movement of the Holy Spirit in revival, but others would oppose such a work with vigor and earnestness.

The pastoral opposition to revivals of which I have just spoken is not merely to extremes or disorders in revival movements (every man of God should join this kind of opposition), but to the genuine work of God itself. Do you find such a statement difficult? Then consider the position of men in the ministry who are wrong before God and who have no intention of changing. What will happen to their work when revival comes? What will happen to their influence and power? What will happen to their income? When Jesus was on earth, it was the Pharisees who were wrong before God and had no intention of changing. It was their work, their positions, and their influence that were threatened. Why should we suppose their reaction in crucifying Christ is any different from the reactions of other religious leaders whose hearts are wrong before God and whose place and position may be lost?

It need not be this way. The appeal of Second Chronicles 7:14 is as much an appeal to pastors as to others: "If My people, which are called by My name, shall humble themselves, and pray, and seek My face, and turn from their wicked ways; then will I hear from heaven, and will forgive their sin, and will heal their land." Let this be clearly affirmed, if pastors will humble themselves, seek the face of God in effectual, fervent prayer, and turn from their wicked, slothful, careless, self-seeking ways, then the God of revival will hear from heaven and will forgive their sins and will heal their land.

Beyond the making right of wrongs in their own personal lives, pastors need to see afresh their own divinely appointed roles in leading the church to revival. In the past century, an entire army of devout pastors was grateful to refer to themselves and one another as "revival men." The names of many of these leaders are still familiar: Asahel Nettleton, Bennet Tyler, Lyman Beecher, Ebenezer Porter, Timothy Dwight, Edward Dorr Griffin, Charles Backus, Jeremiah Hallock, Samuel J. Mills, Joshua Williams, Increase Graves, Ammi R. Robbins, etc. But where is the army of "revival men" today? Pastors by the tens of thousands need to join this volunteer corps of devout men who will not let God go until He blesses.

Pastors need to consider these additional pointed suggestions.

Do not treat your pulpit work as if these were normal times. In days of crisis, act like men in crisis. When there are people floundering in the open sea without a life preserver, there is no value in a homily explaining the comforts and blessedness of the security of a ship. Quickly throw them a rope before they drown. Divest yourself of your fine garments and holy speech and give the sinking sailors a hand before it is too late. This word picture is no exaggeration. There are countless millions sinking forever into a Christless eternity while the Church takes comfort in dry dock. Perhaps the time has come when you should discard all those prepared sermons and, as a dying man, minister to dying men with the fervency of heart and soul the times demand.

Is it sensible to pursue the course of sermons you have planned when the crises on every hand are so great? Can you not go back to the Word of God and find texts well-suited to the days and situation—texts which have the fire of God in them, texts which will arrest men in their downward plunge, texts which will warn the careless of their pending destruction, texts which the Spirit of God Himself can use mightily to revive His Church again? And can you not add to these God-given texts an impassioned soul that burns with zeal for the spiritual well-being of the world? Can you not lay aside many of the heavy responsibilities that fill your normal days, just as you would lay aside your sleep if the neighbor's house were burning in the night, and spend those added hours in crisis prayer, pleading with God to meet you and equip you afresh for the emergency situation into which our world has plunged?

This is no time for self-pity! Stop blaming yourself for all those mistakes of the past. Aren't they under the blood of Jesus. If He has forgiven and forgotten them, what right do you have to keep discouraging yourself by remembering all those faults and weaknesses? Do you really believe Christ? Then act like a believer. Leave yourself behind and get on with the work of God. The very power that raised Jesus from the dead is available in your life to make you a man of revival today. Start to pray and preach like a man of revival.

Live like a man who personally knows the reviving power of God and you will soon see the reviving power of God in lives around you.

For years pastors have been the greatest single human obstacle to revival. Let all that be past history. The years of comfort and ease are past. The crisis is upon us. Let every man of God rise to the occasion! The God who made Jonathan Edwards an instrument of revival in the eighteenth century is prepared to make a "revival man" of you. The same Jesus who gripped the English-speaking world through the feeble life of George Whitefield is now ready to use you also. Will you give Him the opportunity?

CONGREGATIONAL HINDRANCES TO REVIVAL

As the local church can expect to reap the great harvest of revival blessings when it comes, so it must also expect to share heavy responsibilities for hindering the work of God in times of declension preceding revival. Among the most common obstacles to revival are the *five false loves:*

1. The Love of Tradition

Revival and change are almost synonymous terms, and both clearly cut across the grain of traditionalism. There is no way true revival can occur without major changes disrupting and reordering the life of the Church.

The least change in order, procedure, or familiar surroundings can be a great upset to the lover of tradition. Some parishioners don't really seem to care what happens to their church as long as it remains the same. If the morning service when they were a child began with the repetition of the Apostles' Creed, then that's how they want the service to begin now. Hymnbooks worn to tatters must only be changed if the new ones are the same or at least contain the same familiar songs. While preachers can come and go as mere temporary necessities, the new one had better not dare introduce any new elements in the service or any unfamiliar messages in the pulpit. If the church has always issued a Sunday morning altar call, the traditionalists don't want it abandoned no matter how useless it has become. If the church has never had (so far as the traditionalists care to remember) a Sunday morning altar call, woe to that minister who introduces one even if the Spirit of God shows its urgent necessity and several are converted as a result of its introduction. If three hymns are normally sung, the traditionalist will be offended by four. The pattern is all too familiar and needs no further drawing out here. The application, however, is urgent. God Himself is no traditionalist. While God is orderly and dependable, He is always fresh and vital. God never needs a beady-eyed band of tradition-lovers dictating what

He can and cannot do, or how He must and must not do it. If the church runs according to the forms and traditions of men, it will run without the presence and power of God. Without these divine benefits, a church should prepare itself for the grave.

The traditionalist is only fooling himself when he supposes things remain as they always were. Change and decay abound everywhere among the lovers of tradition. What many traditionalists really oppose is not change but observable improvement. The world of the lovers of tradition grows smaller and more decadent with each passing year, but they do not think to oppose this change. It is the bringing in of new life and new ideas that they resist so strongly. Is it any wonder the love of tradition is an enemy of revival? Revival and new life go hand in hand. Revival and visible improvements are partners. Let every church realize that the inordinate love of tradition is a great opponent to revival and cannot be tolerated in the Christian assembly. When the church has slain this love on the altar of sacrifice, a major obstacle to revival will be slain with it.

2. The Love of Disorder

The ordering of priorities according to Scripture and sound spiritual judgment is a discipline in which most churches fail miserably. In studying the program of a typical church, one may often find it impossible to be certain whether it is a business venture, a social club, a political lobby, a neighborhood block party, a sports center, or a nominal religious organization.

Even those churches which are distinctly religious are not always distinctly spiritual. Consider these typical attendance figures: 2,400 persons in attendance on Sunday Morning; 600 in attendance on Sunday evening (when the weather is not too good or not too bad); 60 for prayer meeting. These figures are not for average churches but for thriving centers of passionate evangelical action where Sunday evening services and prayer meetings are still considered vital.

Which is more important to the church: a building program, foreign missions, religious education, recreational and social programs, the worship of God, intercessory prayer, social action, dynamic and strategic witness, or the power and influence of the Holy Spirit? By looking at your church program, can you tell? By looking at your own heart, are you sure of your own priorities?

What priorities are close to the heart of God? (That is the critical question.) Does He care about building programs? Does He care as much about foreign missions as about personal holiness? If God were to step physically into the position of leadership in your church, what changes would occur immediately? If you know what changes He would make, why don't you make those changes for Him? If we know He is not pleased with our ordering of things, how can we persist in the disorder?

What a shocking picture the Church presents to the world. Out of one side of its mouth it declares we are living in the last days and the end of the world is only moments away, while out of the other side of its mouth it calls for massive funds to erect cathedrals and Christian education facilities designed to last for centuries. While it is busy telling men to live like pilgrims passing through this world, the Church is accumulating property and goods as if temporal security were tantamount to godliness. How can the world believe a witness that apparently loves disorder? *self contradt*

When the Church learns to love the things God loves and orders its priorities according to His plan, a major barrier to revival will be broken down.

3. The Love of Brevity

Many congregations do not really seem to care what the preacher says as long as he says it quickly and within the allotted hour. If the murmuring of a typical congregation is suggestive of what they really think, no sin is more awful than that committed by the overtime preacher. What would the Apostle Paul think of being told the service had to be finished within an hour and the sermon could be no more than twenty minutes long? The apostles, the prophets, and the great preachers of the past would all be barred by this ungodly limitation imposed by the lovers of brevity.

Consider this strange phenomenon: the love of brevity seems exclusive; that is to say, it does not apply equally to all things in life but only to spiritual things. The mere thought of a two-and-a-half hour sermon is enough to send shivers of fright and discomfort down the spines of the lovers of brevity, but the anticipation of a four-hour sporting event on Saturday seems to shorten the tedious hours of the working week. People that absolutely cannot sit still for more than an hour in church have been known to spend three-and-a-half hours in a theatre without leaving their seats and entire evenings in front of their television sets without any thoughts of discomfort.

Can the Spirit of God be told to do His work within a prescribed hour? Can the maker of time be advised how much time He is allotted to accomplish His will and purpose in His own Church? Is it even reasonable to suppose a mere hour is in any way a sufficient length of time to devote to the care and nurture of the eternal soul? Even if we could be so foolish as to suppose every Christian attends church every Sunday morning in the year, that would still give only a total of fifty-two hours for the entire year, scarcely more time than a good workman spends each week on his job and less time than some people spend watching television weekly.

The hypocrisy of this love of spiritual brevity is so obvious it is

hard to believe there could be a Christian anywhere in the world
affected by it. But in truth almost every church is in its grip. It is a
rare and wonderful thing to talk with an honest pastor who can
declare perfect liberty in teaching and preaching the Word of God
without regard to time. The church that is free of clock-watchers is
unusual indeed.

When this false love of brevity is swallowed up by the higher
affection of a genuine love for God, one of the most effective barriers
to real ministry in the local church will be lifted and the prospect of
revival wonderfully increased.

4. The Love of Comfortable Truth

There is a time for comfort and a time to be made uncomfortable.
The church that forgets this raises a powerful barrier to revival in its
midst. The Bible abounds in passages designed for the comfort and
security of the believer, and rightly used at the right times, these
Scriptures are to the glory of God and the good of the Church. Used
continually and without regard to the deepest needs of a congregation, comforting truths can be damning.

Many persons attending church services have no desire to be
disturbed or aroused. Pastors in general, in order to satisfy this love
of comfort in their congregations, use great care in preparation of
their sermons to see that no one is aroused or upset. Some, whose
conscience will not let them be completely careless, will preach the
more earnest sermons in the evening service when those that need it
most will be sure to be absent. If indeed, by some slip, they should
happen to disturb some comfortable parishioners, they may even
apologize to the entire congregation. Not content to apologize for
themselves alone, some will even go so far as to apologize for visiting
preachers. It will be a long time before I forget the pastor who,
immediately following my sermon in which it seemed as if a gripping
sense of the Spirit of God became manifest, apologized for what I
said, saying he was sure I did not wish to see anyone aroused or
upset. Is it any wonder the church is declining? When grown men and
women cannot face the facts of spiritual life and death, how can they
even pretend to love the truth?

The love of comfort is closely akin to indifference and can
scarcely be separated from it. The world is perishing but the lover of
comfortable truth says, "Let us sleep on." The forces of wickedness
are mounting on every hand, but these indifferent persons yawn in the
face of facts and say, "Don't trouble us with talk of sin and wrath and
judgment. God is a God of love and mercy and that is enough for us."
"God is a good Father," these indifferent hypocrites piously say.
"Surely He will not let any of His children suffer. There is enough of
sorrow and upset in the world; let us not bring it into the church."

Revival and the exclusive love of comfortable truths are bitter enemies. Churches may fill their padded pews with careless listeners who love the low lights, soft organ tones, and conversational sermons on pleasant subjects, but they will never fill heaven until they declare all the truth of Scripture with the convicting, disturbing power of the Holy Spirit. Where revival prevails, the love of false comfort takes flight. Pampering and coddling the base nature of man is a devilish device the Church must resist. Arousing men from their sin and sloth and firing them with zeal for the kingdom of God can only be accomplished when the Church crucifies its love of comfortable truth and without fear and equivocation stands with God in the declaration of the full counsel of His Word.

5. The Love of Respect

"What will people think?" Here is a question the church should never ask. Its great concern must be, "What does God think?" Which of these two questions really concern you and your church?

Many pastors have been told, in one form or another, "Pastor, this is the '——— Church' and we don't allow that sort of thing here." Perhaps he is told this when proposing to introduce a testimony meeting into the Sunday evening service; maybe this comes up when he suggests a special series of evangelistic meetings. Conceivably, this is the response when he calls for all-day fasting and prayer. Whatever the occasion that prompts the response, it is the problem that lies behind the statement that ought to concern us. Many churches seem far more concerned with their image in the world than with their spiritual effectiveness. They would rather have the respect of men than the favor of God. To be well thought of on earth is more essential in their thinking than to be highly esteemed in heaven.

And it is not just the church as a body that faces this problem. It is also a problem of individual professing Christians within its membership. To be caught weeping over sins during the church service is unthinkable for many. To stand before the congregation and confess one's heinous sins of murmuring and backbiting would require more grace and humility than most church members, including elders, deacons, and Sunday school teachers, have ever known. Many would prefer to be thought righteous than to be righteous. Somehow, having their fellowmen suppose them worthy of membership in a physical church seems more important to many professing Christians than the certain knowledge of sins forgiven and the unceasing experience of God's reviving grace.

There is a tragic element of self-deception in "playing church." The world is not that enamored with '——— Church.' Its disinterest and even disgust are manifested weekly by total absence or careless attendance at its services. No one gains lasting respect from fellow hypocrites; there really is none to gain. To compromise for acclaim is to guarantee rejection. The love of the respect of men is a long-distance ticket to loneliness and despair.

While the Church places the respect of men before the favor of God, it has neither. The love of respect is a slippery path that leads to hell. No individual and no church can afford the luxury of such an error. When the Church is overwhelmed with its desire to do God's will and will not waste its time and energies caring what people think, then a powerful hindrance to revival will be removed.

These false loves have characterized the affections of the Church too long. Now they must go! In their place must stand pure and undefiled love for God.

GENERAL HINDRANCES TO REVIVAL

While certain hindrances to revival specifically affect pastors and other hindrances are particularly the problem of the local church, there are general hindrances to revival that must concern the whole Body of Christ.

1. The Hindrance of Erroneous Interpretation

Have you heard someone say, "These are the last days. No revival of religion can ever again be hoped for. We can only expect things to grow worse and worse"? Obviously such a viewpoint can have a devastating effect on revival interest, but is such a view warranted? We must be sure we understand the use of the expression "last days" in the New Testament. As an illustration of regular usage, consider Hebrews 1:1-3:

> *God, who at sundry times and in divers manners spake in time past unto the fathers by the prophets, hath in these last days spoken unto us by His Son, whom He hath appointed heir of all things, by whom also He made the worlds; who being the bright-ness of His glory, and the express image of His person, and upholding all things by the word of His power, when He had by Himself purged our sins, sat down on the right hand of the majesty on high.*

In this passage, as in a host of others, a contrast is made between "former days" and "latter days"—the "former days" being the Old Testament period and the "latter days" being that period which began in the New Testament and continues to the present. Throughout Christian history the return of Christ has seemed imminent to those who loved His word and His appearing. The Apostles expected Christ to return in their lifetimes, as did a host of reformers, Puritans, settlers of America, pastors, teachers, evangelists, and ordinary

Christians of the past. These all lived in the last days. They understood their days to be the last days as we understand our days to be
the last days. Yet they experienced gracious revivals. While we may
be living in the last days in the fullest and most final sense of that
term, it is also possible that the return of Christ is a century or more
away.

We must face carefully the task assigned to us; certainly it is not
to set the year of Christ's return. That we can safely leave in the
Father's hands. The assignment Jesus gave was, "Occupy till I come"
(Luke 19:13). This assignment was first given in the parable of the
ten talents and clearly teaches the right use of God-given opportunities. If we spend our time and energies calculating the details of
our Lord's coming, we may easily miss opportunities of "occupying till
He comes." What greater opportunity is there than revival?

In the event the return of Christ is yet some distance off, the
Church must be cautious not to be more explicit in making statements concerning it than Scripture. Over the centuries many books
have been written concerning Christ's coming, and some of these
ancient volumes were plain in stating the return would be within the
lifetime of the author. Some of these writers were as convinced as
writers in our own day, but they were wrong and in this way demonstrated themselves to be false prophets. Certainly Christ can come at
any moment, and may come before you finish reading this page, but
His coming could be a thousand years away. We are commanded,
*Therefore be ye also ready: for in such an hour as ye think not the Son
of man cometh* (Matthew 24:44). Making false predictions is not a
good way to make ready.

We must not let our observations on the condition of society and
the degeneration of the hearts of men block our earnest seeking of
God's face. God is as able to send revival now as at any time during
the history of His Church. While on the surface things do seem to be
getting worse and worse, a balanced perspective on history clearly
suggests that the Bible is absolutely right in declaring men of all
times and in all places *deceitful and desperately wicked.* There have
been times in the past when it looked as if the world could not
survive another generation, and yet it did. This may well be the last
generation, but then again, our great-great-grandchildren may be the
ones to see Christ's coming in the air. Since the possibility exists that
this may not be the last generation, we should, with ever increasing
fervency, seek a mighty outpouring of the Spirit of God in revival
blessing for the sake of both our own and future generations and for
the glory of our great God and Savior Jesus Christ.

To hinder revival by arbitrarily announcing that it cannot come
because of the late hour of history in which we live is to abandon our
role as faithful servants of Jesus Christ and to pose as God. If He

chooses to revive us again, who has sufficient authority to say He cannot? Time after time, in the dark seasons of the past, God has stepped into the stream of history and sent revival. Why shouldn't we expect Him to do it again?

2. The Hindrance of Prayerlessness

Prayerlessness must be linked with carelessness. According to James, we *have not* either because we ask not or because we ask amiss (James 4:2-3). No greater hindrance to revival could possibly be pinpointed than the almost unbelievable prayerlessness that exists.

The vast majority of professed Christians seem never to pray for revival at all. Of the handful who pray for it, only a small percentage pray with regularity. Among those who pray with regularity, a minority pray as if they were desperately in earnest. And unfortunately, even some among this slim number are growing weary of asking and are abandoning their divinely appointed task while the hand of God is still preparing the blessing.

This is strange conduct, indeed, in view of the fact that there is little else, besides praying, men can do to bring revival. Prayer is the single most important task God has assigned men in their earthly pilgrimage. Prayer is so vital to the human walk that Jesus Himself devoted extended periods (as much as forty days and nights at one time) to it. Scripture abounds with commands, encouragements, and invitations to pray as well as with illustrations of prayer.

The very heart of the biblical teaching on prayer is fervency and consistency. When men are so earnest that they cannot live without a desired blessing, God is pleased with their attitude and takes delight in their petitions. Halfhearted praying doesn't even produce half-hearted results. It is worse than nothing. In fact, it is an affront against a gracious God. He Himself is earnest. God deals earnestly with people and requires people to deal earnestly with Him.

 Secret prayer for revival is absolutely essential. Men must begin with prayer for the revival of their own souls. They must wrestle with God in their own closets for this needed blessing. When it comes, there will come with it a burden for a larger awakening affecting the whole Church. This prayer for revival must go on unceasingly. It must shape and affect all of life. It must become a burden of major proportions. It is a duty and a privilege not to be abandoned.

Prayer for revival must also become a major part of the prayer life of the local church. It ought to find its way into the public services of worship. It ought to dominate the prayer meetings of the congregation. Prayer for revival in the local church must begin with a focus on the spiritual needs of that fellowship and must include a willingness, even a heartfelt desire, to be "broken" before the Lord. As the Lord begins to stir and move, this prayer for revival must be extended to include the entire Body of Christ. Such prayer, if it is effective, cannot be occasional or insipid. Energy and enthusiasm must be poured into this God-appointed work. Failure to do so is a monstrous hindrance to revival.

A mighty concert of prayer is needed. Prayer meetings for revival should spring up in offices, homes, factories, and schools across the nation. All sectarian interests should be abandoned for the great cause of revival prayer. Men and women of various persuasions and backgrounds must agree on earth as touching this one thing—that they can not and will not live without revival. The God of all mercies can not and will not resist such prayer.

3. The Hindrance of Faithlessness

God hears the prayer of faith. No prayer prevails that comes from the faithless heart. Jesus said,

> *Have faith in God. For verily I say unto you, That whosoever shall say unto this mountain, Be thou removed, and be thou cast into the sea; and shall not doubt in his heart, but shall believe that those things which he saith shall come to pass; he shall have whatsoever he saith. Therefore I say unto you, What things soever ye desire, when ye pray, believe that ye receive them, and ye shall have them (Mark 11:22-24).*

Which is harder—for God to move an entire mountain from its place on land and cast it into the sea or for God to revive His work? Neither! God has no difficulty with either one. We are the ones with difficulties. We find it almost impossible to truly believe that God will do remarkable things for us. In consequence, much of our praying is as nothing.

The prayer of faith is linked with the knowledge of the will of God. If you do not know that revival is God's will you may pray with the feeble hope God will be merciful enough to revive His people again, but your prayers will lack the confidence necessary for success.

Two questions must be asked concerning revival. First, "Will revival be to the glory of God?" If revival cannot enhance that glory, then it is of a doubtful nature. But, can you imagine anything that would bring more glory to God than a wonderful, deep, wide, and glorious revival that would turn millions of backsliders into fervent Christians and bring countless unbelievers into a saving relationship with Jesus Christ? The Psalmist's often repeated prayer reflects this truth: "Revive us again: that Thy people may rejoice in Thee" (Psalm 85:6). The glory of God will be wonderfully increased by revival, so from this standpoint, at least, we can pray with confidence.

Second, "Will revival genuinely advance the work of Christ on earth?" or "Will it significantly help to answer the petition, 'Thy will be done on earth, as it is in heaven'?" Again we might ask, "Can anything other than revival do so much to accomplish God's will and purpose?" I am personally unaware of anything more nearly in line with the heart and purpose of God than the revival of His work. Surely prayer for revival is within the will of God and can be lifted heavenward with great confidence and faith.

Do you pray in faith for revival? The failure to do so is a shameful hindrance to the work of God on earth. How can you justify it?

Chapter Seven

Will
the Fruits
of Revival
Last?

They who have no keen stomachs which want to be fed and satiated with the milk of the Word, are but so many dead carcasses or skins stuffed with rotten bones. It would be the same thing to desire the naturally dead to quit their graves, as to desire such to leave their sins. Well may our land be compared to Golgotha, a place full of dead men's skulls. It is melancholy to think that there are in it many thousands of miserable souls, dead in sins and dead in affections, who have no spiritual taste for God's Word or the least hankering after it. If they have a mealy-mouthed priest to read a little unto them now and then, they count themselves very fortunate, as if Elisha's staff was sufficient to raise the dead child to life without Elisha himself. They imagine that the Word is able to give life of itself, and hence they seek not the Spirit of the Lord. If they had even Judas for their teacher, they would be satisfied with him and would not go a step farther to hear Paul. Woe is me that I am obliged to declare that the ministers who reprove them the least for their sins, and detain them for the shortest while in the churches, are held in the highest estimation by them. Their sentiments are very different from the sentiments of those worthies of old, who delighted in the law of the Lord and in His law meditated day and night: who "Departed not from the temple, but served God with fastings and prayers night and day." They plainly show that they have no relish for God's Word and that they do not desire it as newborn babes.

Daniel Rowland, Llangeitho, Wales

Will the Fruits of Revival Last?

It is almost impossible to talk about revival without talking about its fruits. Christians may appear to live for years without any appreciable changes in their personal lives, but when revival comes, the changes will be frequent and often radical. Whole congregations and entire denominations may be redirected and renewed when the Spirit of God is poured out in revival blessings. There is no way to predict the depth, breadth, or height of revival influence, but we can be sure dramatic changes will accompany it.

Two classes of individuals will be most directly affected by the revival: first, a wonderful group of new converts will be brought into the church; second, hosts of persons formerly in various stages of backsliding will be powerfully and beautifully reclaimed. In order that the blessings of revival may be especially preserved among these two classes of individuals, I invite their particular attention at this time.

Every fruit farmer is aware of the delicate nature of his work at particular seasons of the year, especially at the time of harvest. All the results of good husbandry can be spoiled if the ripened crop is picked, packed, and shipped like coal. A splendid harvest deserves the greatest possible care so that none of the fruit is damaged or lost. In the same way, the fruits of revival must be as carefully handled as golden peaches or fragrant nectarines. To do otherwise is absurd.

If the fruit of revival is to be preserved, it is very important for the recipients of revival blessing to consider carefully the truths best calculated to improve their spiritual experience. Because of the fragile nature of true revival, carelessness at this point can result in much damage and loss.

INSTRUCTIONS FOR NEW CONVERTS

I now urge the careful attention of those who find themselves hopeful new converts of the revival. Not all "converts" of revival movements have lasted. Some have fallen away. These words of instruction are specifically designed to assist you in putting down deep roots and in pressing upward in your newly found relationship with Jesus Christ. I begin by asking you to:

Verify Your Position In Christ.

Notice I have used the expression, "hopeful new converts" of the revival. If there is anything faulty about your relationship with Christ, now is the time to discover and correct it. In the heat of revival it is possible for someone to suppose he has become a Christian only to discover at a later date that he was not converted at all.

In concluding His Sermon on the Mount (Matthew 5-7) Jesus gave a parable every person hopefully converted in a revival needs to consider thoughtfully:

> *Whosoever heareth these sayings of Mine, and doeth them, I will liken him unto a wise man, which built his house upon a rock: and the rain descended, and the floods came, and the winds blew, and beat upon that house; and it fell not: for it was founded upon a rock. And every one that heareth these sayings of mine, and doeth them not, shall be likened unto a foolish man, which built his house upon the sand: and the rain descended, and the floods came, and the winds blew, and beat upon that house; and it fell: and great was the fall of it (7:24-27).*

No one can build a house upon the rock who has not first learned where rock is. That is your task now. What if the next several months are spent building your spiritual house, but when the winds and rains of adversity come you discover it is all built upon sand? In the illustration Jesus gives, the sand foundation is compared with hearing the Word of God but not really acting upon it. The great test of your entire conversion experience and all that follows as a professed Christian is and will be your faithful adherence to the Word of God. Your entire experience to date must be tested by the Bible, and your entire Christian life must be structured by this same unchanging standard. If your experience is judged unsound biblically, it has no lasting value no matter how exciting it seemed or how good it made you feel at the time. You cannot be certain of your own relationship with Christ by comparing it with other professing Christians around you. Some of them may have built their houses upon sand also. Now is the time to find bedrock and to lay a foundation that will stand for eternity.

A genuine conversion occurs when Jesus Christ is sincerely believed. "He that believeth on the Son hath everlasting life: and he that believeth not the Son shall not see life; but the wrath of God abideth on him" (John 3:36). The dividing line between true and false believers is genuine faith in Christ: "But without faith it is impossible to please Him: for he that cometh to God must believe that He is, and that He is a rewarder of them that diligently seek Him" (Hebrews 11:6). If you will study the entire eleventh chapter of Hebrews, you will discover that every person who is described there as having faith acted on the basis of that faith. Saving faith is not a passive acknowledgement of the existence of God or of the saving merits of the shed blood of Jesus Christ, but an active response as expressed in the words "diligently seek." When Jesus Christ is really believed, appropriate action follows. Believing Jesus requires believing what He says. Believing what He says will mean doing what He says. The action produced by faith gives visible evidence of the presence of faith. Without the action there is no real evidence that faith exists. This is the very reason James said, "Even so faith, if it hath not works, is dead, being alone. Yea, a man may say, Thou hast faith, and I have works: shew me thy faith without thy works, and I will shew thee my faith by my works. Thou believest that there is one God; thou doest well: the devils also believe, and tremble. But wilt thou know, O vain man, that faith without works is dead?" (2:17-20).

The Bible declares that Jesus Christ is Lord. Saving faith enables a person not only to acknowledge the Lordship of Christ but to submit to it. When Jesus Christ becomes Lord of an individual's life, a genuine conversion occurs. If Christ is not Lord, no true conversion exists despite formula prayers that may have been uttered, overt physical responses made, or feelings and emotions stirred. Here and now you can accurately test the validity of your own conversion experience by determining if Jesus Christ is really your Lord. If he is not Lord, nothing that you have felt or experienced is sufficient. If you cling to a precious experience but miss the Lordship of Christ, a terrible day of reckoning is still before you. If you content yourself with the feeble prayers you have uttered and the overt responses you have made and persist in remaining unyielded to Christ, you are yet in your sins no matter what men may say to the contrary.

To assist you in being certain of the Lordship of Jesus Christ in your life, may I request your careful consideration of the following elementary truths:

1. Your personal sin is so great that unless you are delivered from it you are in eternal trouble. The biblical law is, "The soul that sinneth, it shall die" (Ezekiel 18:20a). Every sin you have committed bears the penalty of eternal death. The number of your sins or the degree of terribleness of your sins does not alter the penalty. A single sin earns this penalty; a seemingly little sin earns this penalty; a childish sin earns this penalty. This death is eternal separation from God. This separation was earned the very first time you sinned and remains in force until the penalty is paid. There is no room here for argument or debate. It is a plain biblical fact.

2. If this penalty of sin is to be paid, someone other than yourself must pay it. There is no price at your command sufficient to pay this penalty. Being already under the just sentence of death because of sin, there is no way you can escape the consequences. No good deeds or acts of righteousness have sufficient value to pay such a debt. Some foolish persons think their good deeds and their evil deeds will be placed in a balance by God. Because they believe their good is certain to outweigh their evil, they are confident "everything will turn out all right in the end." Such nonsense clearly demonstrates a foundation of sand. There is only one method by which the debt of sin can be satisfied—the shedding of innocent blood. You have no innocent blood to shed and thus can never hope to overcome the problem of your own sin or escape its penalty.

3. Jesus Christ came into the world as the innocent Lamb of God. He lived without sin. No curse of the law rested upon Him. When Jesus Christ died on the cross, He died not having committed a single sin. He died, not for His own sins, but for yours. He died in your place. He took your sins upon Himself and paid your debt. His innocent blood was shed for you. In His death Jesus Christ made a substitutionary atonement; that is, the Lamb of God who knew no sin was made sin for you that you might be made "the righteousness of God in Him" (Second Corinthians 5:21). Apart from this substitution-ary death of Christ there is no hope. In His death are forgiveness of sins and eternal life.

4. When through the aid of the Holy Spirit these simple truths become clear and are definitely accepted as Gospel facts, the sinner becomes aware that a response to this substitutionary death is mandatory. The great question then becomes, "What response is required?" That response is clearly stated by Paul to the keeper of the jail at Philippi, "Believe on the Lord Jesus Christ, and thou shalt be saved..." (Acts 16:31). Notice, it is not merely, "Believe on Jesus" or "Believe on Jesus Christ," but "Believe on the Lord Jesus Christ." Here, in simple language, is the answer to, "What must I do to be saved?" There is one acceptable response to the death of Jesus Christ in your place—submission to His Lordship. Those who have been genuinely converted are those who have truly received Jesus Christ as Lord. Stated in another way, conversion occurs when an exchange of life takes place—the sinner yields his life of sin and self to the Lord Jesus Christ who in turn imparts His life of righteousness. The sinner abandons the throne of his life and the Lord Jesus Christ takes command. This is biblical conversion and anything else is a disap-pointing substitute.

Obviously, it is possible to have a happy revival "experience" without ever yielding to Christ's Lordship. But any experience, no matter how fervent or joyous, which does not result in Jesus Christ becoming Lord of your life is a sand castle soon to be dissolved in the waves of reality. Is your spiritual house built on solid rock or on shifting sand?

5. The new convert should also realize there is a genuine biblical assurance for those who have truly believed the Lord Jesus Christ. In Romans eight we are told, "Ye have not received the spirit of bondage again to fear; but ye have received the Spirit of adoption, whereby we cry, Abba, Father [Father my Father]. The Spirit itself [Himself] beareth witness with our spirit, that we are the children of God: and if children, then heirs; heirs of God, and joint-heirs with Christ..." (verses 15-17). When faith is placed in the Lord Jesus Christ, the Holy Spirit of God gives us inward witness of the changed relationship which has occurred. This "witness of the Spirit" is the privilege of every true believer, but the nature of the assurance is not such that it is always present to the same degree. If you find some wavering in this inner witness, then apply these additional biblical tests of your standing with God:

a) A true follower of Christ has a genuine love for others. The First Epistle of John is rich in help on this subject. Consider these verses:

> *If a man say, I love God, and hateth his brother, he is a liar: for he that loveth not his brother whom he hath seen, how can he love God whom he hath not seen? And this commandment have we from Him, That he who loveth God love his brother also* (4:20,21).

Ponder too:

> *Hereby perceive we the love of God, because He laid down His life for us: and we ought to lay down our lives for the brethren. But whoso hath this world's good, and seeth his brother have need, and shutteth up his bowels of compassion from him, how dwelleth the love of God in him? My little children, let us not love in word, neither in tongue; but in deed and in truth. And hereby we know that we are of the truth, and shall assure our hearts before Him"* (First John 3:16-19).

b) A true follower of Christ has a spirit of forgiveness toward those who have injured and wronged him. The Scripture is clear on this point: "If you forgive men their trespasses, your heavenly Father will also forgive you: But if ye forgive not men their trespasses, neither will your Father forgive your trespasses" (Matthew 6:14,15).

c) A true follower of Christ will have an earnest yearning to be free of all sin. There is no way the truly born of God can go on living in the pleasures of sin: "Whosoever is born of God doth not [practice] sin" (First John 3:9). While some sin remains in the child of God, it is a loathsome source of agony and remorse and the constant cause of the true believer's desire for deliverance.

These biblical tests, along with the inner witness of the Spirit, should amply demonstrate the genuineness of your conversion experience. But suppose you fail the test and realize that all is not well! Should you be discouraged? Should you consider backing away from your new interest in spiritual things? Certainly not! The remedy is to think again of the problem of your personal sin. Carefully face the awful penalty already earned. See Jesus Christ dying in your place on that cursed cross. Do you not have sufficient reason to cast yourself completely upon Christ and yield totally to His Lordship? Then do it!

Solidify Your Position In Christ

When you are certain of the Lordship of Jesus Christ in your life, it is time to solidify your position as a child of God. I suggest four separate steps:

1. Confess the Lord Jesus Christ with your own mouth. Every genuine revival convert must make an open confession of Jesus Christ as Lord:

> *If thou shalt confess with thy mouth the Lord Jesus, and shalt believe in thine heart that God hath raised Him from the dead, thou shalt be saved. For with the heart man believeth unto righteousness; and with the mouth confession is made unto salvation (Romans 10:9,10).*

Secret Christians are a figment of the imagination. If you are ashamed of Jesus Christ your Lord, He will be ashamed of you (Luke 9:26).

Let the world know what the Savior has done for you. This biblical requirement is as much for your benefit as anything else. If no one knows of your commitment to the Lord Jesus, it will be much harder for you to live for His glory than if you openly acknowledge Him. Take your public stand without regard to ridicule or shame and you will find you do not stand alone. The Lord Himself will be with you.

2. Be baptized in water. From the time of the ministry of John the Baptist until the present, water baptism has stood for an outward sign of an inward change. In the waters of baptism one visibly expresses his death to self and his resurrection to newness of life in Christ the Lord. In addition to being an important outward sign, baptism is also an inward means of grace for spiritual growth and stability.

3. Seek fellowship in a church. It is highly improbable that any church is totally perfect, but every Bible-preaching, Christ-centered church is divinely ordained by God and used by Him. True fellowship with Jesus Christ will bring you into fellowship with every other true believer. Waste no time in finding a local church where you can commit yourself to the disciplines and ministries of that fellowship. Make sure that the church to which you attach yourself is faithful in teaching, preaching, and living by the Word of God. No spiritual profit can be expected from church fellowship with unbelievers. Also, make sure there is an earnest, active prayer meeting in the church in which you can take a vital part. Avoid any church that does not have a strong commitment to prayer.

4. Find some useful work to do for Christ. Your own commitment to the Lord will be greatly enriched as you live out your life in service to others. Carefully consider your God-given talents, and find a place of service where your abilities will be utilized and your spiritual muscles stretched. Let your service be according to your state of grace. The beginner in the faith is not called upon to teach and preach. The office of the elder in the church is reserved for men of spiritual maturity. Start with a task that fits your present circumstances, and advance in service as you advance in the knowledge and likeness of Christ.

Improve Your Position In Christ

Growth is mandatory. In the physical world, the baby that does not grow is a source of concern and pity. So is the spiritually stunted convert. Your personal growth in grace and in the knowledge of Jesus Christ should be observable both to yourself and to others.

There are some old-fashioned biblical terms which need to be clarified immediately. The word *salvation* is like a great umbrella. It covers three separate and distinct aspects of God's work of grace in you. For every true believer, the first aspect has already been completed—*justification*. We are justified by faith. The moment true faith is placed in the Lord Jesus Christ, justification occurs. At that moment sin is pardoned and eternal life is received. The justified sinner is treated by God as if he had never sinned, for the very righteousness of Jesus Christ covers him.

The second aspect of salvation, however, is not accomplished in a moment of time, but is progressive. It is called *sanctification*. Leaving it for a moment, let me name the final aspect of this wonderful work of salvation—*glorification*. Glorification occurs the moment we enter the eternal presence of our Lord Jesus Christ in heaven: "We know that, when He shall appear, we shall be like Him; for we shall see Him as He is" (First John 3:2b). Two of these steps are accomplished without cost to us or great effort on our part—justification and glorification; the third is accomplished with great difficulty. Notice First Peter 4:18: "If the righteous scarcely [with difficulty] be saved, where shall the ungodly and sinner appear?" The righteous are those already justified, who shall certainly be glorified, but who are now experiencing the gracious work of sanctification with great difficulty. In the context of this passage it is clear that the sufferings and persecutions which the believer experiences pose great difficulty, for it is not normal for any of us to wish to experience pain. Sanctification, which literally speaks of "setting apart for a holy purpose," is sure to bring us into the realm of persecution and difficulty. This is forever occurring in the life of the believer and necessitates that we daily count ourselves dead to sin and alive to God through Jesus Christ our Lord (Romans 6:11). God's intent is to perfect us in the things concerning Christ and that which we must endure as growing believers is serving this end. Sometimes, in the weakness of our lives, we are tempted to seize the controls and ease the pain of sanctification, but we must continually remain off the throne of our hearts and let Christ reign there.

Yet we must not err in thinking that Christ justifies us and glorifies us but that we sanctify ourselves. Jesus Christ is our justifier, our sanctifier and our glorifier or final redemption. Notice First Corinthians 1:30: "But of Him are ye in Christ Jesus, who of God is made unto us wisdom, and righteousness, and sanctification, and redemption." The precious teaching of this verse is made much clearer by a change in punctuation: "But of Him are ye in Christ Jesus, who of God is made unto us wisdom: righteousness, sanctification and redemption." This same effect is accomplished in some translations by the insertion of a word: "But of Him are ye in Christ Jesus, who of God is made unto us wisdom *even* righteousness, sanctification and redemption." The focus on wisdom in this passage points to the fact that a complete salvation was purchased by Christ in His death, burial and resurrection. Through faith we are justified; through faith we are sanctified; through faith we are glorified.

It is in keeping with correct biblical language to describe ourselves as "being saved." We have been saved from the penalty of sin in *justification.* We are here and now being saved from the power of sin in *sanctification.* We shall be saved from the presence of sin in *glorification.*

With these elementary truths of Scripture in your thinking, I urge you to pursue further, with great care, this daily growth in sanctification by carefully considering and applying the series of instructions that follow that are directed to those persons recently reclaimed from backsliding. Remember, it is impossible for you to stand still in the Christian life. If you do not move forward you will surely slide backward.

INSTRUCTIONS FOR REVIVED BELIEVERS

I now invite the special attention of those professing Christians who have found themselves the subjects of special reviving grace. By your past experience you have already established the ease with which you can backslide. It is essential that you lay with care the foundation of a life of constant spiritual growth and increasing spiritual power and fruit. Failure to do so may bring unfortunate results. Consider this sober warning urged by Jesus Himself:

> When the unclean spirit is gone out of a man, he walketh through dry places, seeking rest, and findeth none. Then he saith, I will return into my house from whence I came out; and when he is come, he findeth it empty, swept, and garnished. Then goeth he, and taketh with himself seven other spirits more wicked than himself, and they enter in and dwell there: and the last state of that man is worse than the first. Even so shall it be also unto this wicked generation (Matthew 12:43-45).

You can be absolutely certain Satan will not share your newly restored joy in Christ. If there is any way he can blight your spiritual life, he will. As Christ's statement so plainly warns, the last state will be "worse than the first." Failure to fill your life with the precious things of Jesus Christ will leave you open to a new influx of evil far greater than any you have ever known. Don't let this happen to you.

1. Refuse at all times to compromise, even in the slightest degree, the Lordship of Christ. He is Lord! You dare not interfere again with His Lordship. You began your earlier career of backsliding by allowing your own interests to crowd Christ out of your life. Whereas you professed Him as Lord, in practice He was not Lord of all and therefore not Lord at all. You must not let this happen again. Keep Christ upon the throne of your life. Do not struggle with Him for authority. In every single instance yield to Him and let Him be Lord and Master. He has this right since He purchased you with His own blood. He is better equipped for this position than you are since He knows the end from the beginning and every turn of the road in between. He has your interest at heart and is sure to guard your welfare more carefully than you will yourself.

The unchanging God is not subject to fits of passion or fluctuations in loyalties. As the Creator of all, He has a better understanding of the needs and truest pleasures of His creation than the created could possibly have. As the God of all mercies, He can be relied upon to fill all the deficiencies of your character and to smooth all the sharp edges of your personality. When He is fully in control of your life, you will reap a bountiful harvest of peace, joy, and usefulness.

If you challenge the Lordship of Jesus Christ in your life, He will yield, for He is not the Lord of unwilling subjects. If you murmur against His leadership, you may grieve His blessed Holy Spirit and He may draw back and then you find yourself once more in the quagmire of doubt and uncertainty. Jesus Christ is Lord. Accept this joyfully! Learn to delight in complete submission to Him. Enjoy the true freedom that comes from surrender. While He is Lord, the fruits of revival will remain in your life, enriching not only you but also all those around you.

   2. Do not consider temptations. In Ephesians 1:4 it is clear that God has elected (chosen) us to be holy. We must not consider any alternatives even for a fleeting moment. Backsliding begins by giving consideration to evil. If the tempted individual so much as ponders the temptation, the likelihood of his fall is vastly increased. Consider Jesus when He was tempted by the devil in the wilderness. Did He weigh the temptations? Did He consider the pros and cons of the devil's offers? Absolutely not! Jesus did not allow the tempter's dazzle to captivate His mind or lure His fancy even for a moment. With a word of Scripture and a sharp command, Jesus put the devil to flight.

   After a person is elected to an office, does he have the right to consider whether or not he will do the job for which he was elected? If there were any question about whether or not he was going to do the job, that question should have been considered and answered prior to the election. Having accepted the nomination, having run for the office, having been elected to the position, he has a clear task— do the job, filling the office to which he has been elected. So it is with our election to holiness. We have no business considering whether or not to be holy. God has elected us to holiness without any options otherwise. The believer has no lawful choice to be anything but holy.

   Tragically, many professing Christians do not face temptation this way. When the devil lures them toward sin, they consider whether or not to indulge. Perhaps they weigh the issue: "If I do this little thing, will it really matter? Would God really care if I had this little extra pleasure? Even if it isn't exactly right, it can't really do me any great harm." In weighing temptation you assume there is a choice, and in considering that choice, you are making your position very vulnerable. Instead of considering the temptation, you ought to say, "Get out of here Satan. I have been elected to holiness and have neither the time nor the right to consider your proposal."

   This same essential truth is taught in Romans six:

> *Likewise reckon ye also yourselves to be dead indeed unto sin, but alive unto God through Jesus Christ our Lord. Let not sin therefore reign in your mortal body, that ye should obey it in the*

lusts thereof. Neither yield ye your members as instruments of unrighteousness unto sin: but yield yourselves unto God, as those that are alive from the dead, and your members as instruments of righteousness unto God (verses 11-13).

If we consider ourselves "dead to sin," we will not weigh the temptations and consider them. If we know that we are "alive unto God," we know we have all the power we need to be holy. When Christ elected you to holiness, He took away your right to sin. Accept this fact and live victoriously!

3. Establish definite habits of prayer and do not depart from them. During your days of backsliding, prayer was a victim. Do not let it happen again. Prayer must not be thought of as a good, but nonessential part of life. Prayer is as important to you as food and water. You must give as much diligence to preparing for prayer and engaging in it as you give to any other necessity of life. Prayer on the run is surely important but absolutely insufficient. Specific, extended daily periods must be set aside for communion with God. Failure to do so will seriously compromise the result of revival in your life.

Be absolutely rigid in appointing prime time for this most important work. Do not wait until the tag end of the day, when you are too tired to prevail upon God. Pick a key hour when you are at your best and devote this time to meeting God in prayer.

Do not let the cares of life, the needs of family, the press of business, or the urgent clamor of the world steal from you the most vital part of every day. Give it to God with regularity. Give it with increasing earnestness. Give it with all your heart. The God who invites you to meet Him in prayer will see that your time is well spent.

Prayer is not always simple and easy. It can be the hardest task you ever face. Faithfully honoring your time of prayer can be very costly. Sometime, when you are trying to pray and the heavens seem shut against you, it is certain the devil will whisper in your ear and by one suggestion or another encourage you to abandon this seemingly impossible task. He may suggest God is offended and will not listen to you. He may intimate that your own lack of earnestness is your undoing. Whatever form his suggestions take, remember your commitment to pray and refuse to be discouraged. If heaven seems forever sealed against you, keep on praying. If your heart feels dull, keep on praying. If the ongoing spiritual struggle seems too much and you want to quit, don't. Pray when you feel like praying, and pray when you don't. Pray both when God Himself seems to sit on the edge of His throne in eagerness to hear you, and pray when the presence of God seems totally obscured. Pray when you have vigor and joy in your soul, and pray when there isn't enough spiritual energy left in you to enable you to lift your face heavenward. If the devil can defeat you in your prayer life, he can defeat you everywhere else as well and will brag of his victory. Do not give your enemy this opportunity.

When you pray, remember you are coming to the King. Come before Him with reverence. But also remember that you are coming to your King. Do not be afraid to bring great requests to Him; He is able to fulfill them. Do not shy from bringing little personal concerns; He is interested. No king in any earthly realm ever delighted as much in his subjects as Christ delights in you. He wants you to meet Him at His throne. The King will be there waiting. Do not fail Him!

4. Avoid being a spoon-fed Christian. If the fruits of revival are to ripen in your life, you must personally get into the Word of God. During the days of your backsliding it is understandable that you were content to let others feed you little tidbits from the Bible, but as a revived believer, this practice must not continue.

If you have not already done so, secure a good study edition of the Bible. Be sure it is a direct translation from the original languages in which the Scriptures were written and not someone's paraphrase. Get a Bible with a good quality paper and binding that will give you long and excellent service. A Bible that has technical, historical and geographical helps is advisable, but avoid Bibles that include interpretative notes along with the text. You must focus on the Word of God, not another person's understanding of it. A Bible with cross references, maps, and a concordance will be very helpful in a serious program of Bible study.

The physical book itself is not sacred, although the Word of God of which it consists certainly is. Reverence for the Bible should never keep you from its blessings. Don't hesitate to mark your Bible. A system of underlining and note-taking can be wonderfully useful in mastering God's Word.

It is important to set aside time each day for Bible study. While you should plan to read through the entire Bible, it is more important that each session with the Word of God be spiritually profitable than that you cover a certain number of chapters. Be faithful in this Bible work. Don't let other interests or responsibilities crowd it out of your schedule.

Determine to act promptly on the things God teaches you from His Word. We are not called to be mere readers of the Word but doers also. As you read, keep asking, "Is there something here God wants me to do?" Read to affect your life. Read to learn how to practice living the Christian life.

Memorize Scripture. The Psalmist said, "Thy Word have I hid in mine heart, that I might not sin against Thee" (Psalm 119:11). If you fill your mind and heart with Scripture, you will find it is better than carrying a banquet table around with you. By having it in mind, you can meditate upon it day and night. There is scarcely anything you can do for your soul that will bear more fruit than systematic memorization of the Bible.

Seek to master whole portions of Scripture. Take a New Testament book and study it until you understand every portion of it and have faithfully carried out all it calls upon you to do. Go over and over the same portions until they become a vital part of your life.

There are plenty of professing Christians who are content to be spoon-fed. Refuse to be part of that undernourished segment of the Church. Press on to the "fullness of the stature of Christ." The Bible was given to you for this very purpose.

5. Allow no carry-over of wrongs. A major feature of backsliding is the accumulation of evil. Wrong must be dealt with on a daily basis. The very principle Paul emphasized regarding anger (Ephesians 4:26,27) should be laid down as a fundamental tenet of your entire life: "Let not the sun go down upon your wrath: neither give place to the devil." Every Christian sins, but no Christian should allow the sun to go down while that sin remains unconfessed and unforsaken.

Unconfessed sin is like a snowball rolling downhill—it gathers as it rolls and grows with every turn, Sin must be dealt with when it occurs. If you give place in your life to one small sin, that sin will make room for another. Those two sins, working together, will make room for still more. The backslider does not go from a point of spiritual strength to spiritual defeat in a single stroke. It is the cumulative effect of unconfessed and unforsaken sins that eventually carries all before it as an avalanche, burying the backslider beneath its crushing weight.

Through regular prayer and diligent study of Scripture, it is possible to maintain spiritual sensitivity and to keep the Christian conscience functioning at its highest level. If dealt with immediately, sin can do nothing to numb the conscience or the sap spiritual vigor. However, a single sin allowed to remain in the heart overnight poses a serious threat to the entire spiritual life.

Scripture teaches the urgent necessity of maintaining pure minds and hearts: "If we confess our sins, [God] is faithful and just to forgive us our sins, and to cleanse us from all unrighteousness" (First John 1:9). If we "cover our sins," we "shall not prosper" (Proverbs 28:13). Whenever sin is left in the life, even for a brief period, the tendency is to cover it lest it prove to be an outward source of embarrassment or shame. But what is covered from men's eyes can never be hid from the all-seeing eyes of God. In the darkness of its covering, it festers and grows. If allowed to remain, it will permeate a person's life like a terrible cancer.

If you faithfully practice repentance from sin, you will know the continual thrill of walking with the Lord in the "light of His Word," and the revival which has so graciously brought you to this moment of joy will live on in you in unending power.

6. Keep your eyes on Jesus. No one else is your pattern. If you keep looking to Jesus, you will never be disappointed. He won't fail you! There is no danger of Christ being two-faced! He is no hypocrite! He doesn't stumble and fall! He doesn't set a bad example! He doesn't engage in questionable activity! He will never lead you astray! He is always the same!

If you are a people-watcher, you are in danger of disappointment. Even the most devout Christians sometimes seem to be incorrigible, thankless, and unlike Christ. If you watch saints, you will see variety. Sometimes you will be deeply impressed with their saintliness, and other times you will wonder how they can even name the name of Christ and be so sinful. In watching other Christians, you may occasionally be inspired to great heights, but as often as not you will be driven to the pit of discouragement. Saint-watching is a dangerous business, but watching Christ is not.

Jesus is the great example. There is nothing you are called by God to do that Jesus cannot show you how to achieve. He is the "express image" of God's person. All the good and wonderful things we find in God are reflected in Jesus Christ. All that God calls His followers to be, Jesus is already. Fasten your eyes upon Him. Let His life be your pattern and His wonderful power your strength.

Every person is responsible for his own conduct. If a brother falls into sin, that is no excuse for you. If you see hypocrites in the church, that does not give you an excuse to stay away. You will never be called to answer for their sins. It is between you and Christ. Keep your eyes fixed upon Him at all times and in all places; in so doing, you will let the fire of revival now burning in your soul grow even hotter.

7. Take frequent inventory of yourself. God has revived you for a purpose. He could have left you in a backslidden condition but He did not. He has graciously warmed your heart and given you a new sense of His presence and joy. Do not take these benefits for granted. Be ever asking, "Is Jesus really pleased with me today?"

During the days of your backsliding, you were anything but zealous about pleasing the Lord. If you pleased yourself it seemed sufficient, but that attitude cannot be tolerated now. You no longer have the right to ask yourself, "Am I pleased?" These days the great overwhelming question of your life must be, "Is He pleased?"

Are you making the spiritual progress He intended? I cannot answer that question for you nor can any other person. This is between you and God. Learn to face this question candidly, and if you find the progress is not what it should be, press on immediately to greater growth and victory.

Learn to ask the Lord to search you. If this self-examination is solely introspective, you may miss some glaring errors or discourage yourself in the process. Let the words of David aid you, "Search me, O God, and know my heart: try me, and know my thoughts: and see if there be any wicked way in me, and lead me in the way everlasting" (Psalm 139:23,24). If aided in your inventory-taking by the Holy Spirit, you can be confident that not only will secret faults come to light, but also overcoming power will be given as needed. God is even more anxious to make a great Christian out of you than you are to become one.

Do not be discouraged when you fail. God fully understands. His love for you will not be altered. Remember that God's love is not based on our conduct. God loved you while you were deep in sins, and that love is not going to cease just because your Christian progress is less than hoped for. God forgives repeated failures. We must learn to forgive in ourselves what He has already forgiven. Far more important than absolute outward perfection is a heart that earnestly seeks after God. David failed miserably in his behavior, but still is described as "a man after God's own heart." Let this same blessed trait characterize all your future days.

8. Keep firm control on your tongue at all times. In the third chapter of James, we are given considerable help in this task. Great ships, we are told, are turned about by very small rudders, and horses are guided by bits in their mouths. So the tongue, a very small member in proportion to the rest of the body, has great capacity. In a moment's time it can destroy relationships that took years to build and then turn right around and comfort someone else in the deepest griefs known to mankind.

The best way to control the tongue is to control its guidance system. Jesus said, "Out of the abundance of the heart the mouth speaketh" (Matthew 12:34). What's inside a person comes out. If the heart is full of bitterness, the tongue will express it. If the heart feels jealousy, the tongue will describe it. If the heart is bursting with joy, the tongue will make music. If the heart is enveloped in love, the tongue will entwine that love around others.

A murmuring, complaining spirit is as sure a sign of backsliding as the spirit of genuine praise and thanksgiving is of spiritual strength and vigor.

Matthew fifteen records that the scribes and Pharisees questioned Jesus about His disciples, who ate their bread without first washing their hands. After pressing these religious leaders on their willingness to transgress the commandments of God by their own traditions, Jesus rebuked them declaring, "Ye hypocrites, well did Esaias prophesy of you, saying, This people draweth nigh unto Me with their mouth, and honoureth Me with their lips; but their heart is far from

Me. But in vain they do worship Me, teaching for doctrines the commandments of men" (verses 7-9). Then Jesus called the multitude around Him and said, "Hear and understand: Not that which goeth into the mouth defileth a man; but that which cometh out of the mouth, this defileth a man" (verses 10-11). There is no way a person with an evil heart can speak good, nor is there any way a truly good heart can speak evil. Thus we are urged, "Keep thy heart with all diligence; for out of it are the issues of life" (Proverbs 4:23). Your stature as a man or as a woman of God will be largely determined by how you use your tongue.

Here is a remarkable statement, "Out of the same mouth proceedeth blessing and cursing." James vehemently declares, "My brethren, these things ought not so to be. Doth a fountain send forth at the same place sweet water and bitter? Can the fig tree, my brethren, bear olive berries? either a vine figs? so can no fountain both yield salt water and fresh" (James 3:10-12). By the power of the Spirit of God in your life, keep that unruly and dangerous implement—the tongue—under control at all times.

9. Engage regularly in sacrificial service and good works. It cost God a great deal to redeem you. The blood of Jesus Christ was an immense price to pay for your salvation. See that your lifestyle is a constant demonstration to God of your genuine thankfulness. Not for one moment must you allow yourself to think that by these works you are securing salvation or adding to it. What Jesus Christ did on the cross in your place is sufficient and requires no contribution on your part. Yet, you are saved for a purpose, and part of that purpose is that you might serve the living God here and now on this earth.

People in a backslidden condition are rendered spiritually useless. No feeble works on their part are acceptable to God. But, now that you have been revived, you can be an effective instrument of good. If you let the Holy Spirit work through you, you will be delighted to observe the gracious benefits of your own labors.

Serve God by praising Him. Let Him know how grateful you are to be reclaimed.

Serve God by witnessing to others of His wonderful grace. Let them know how merciful the Lord has been in bringing you back from your backsliding.

Serve God by praying for others around you. Many can be won for Christ by prayer.

Serve God by teaching others the very truths you yourself are learning from the Scriptures. They need it greatly.

Serve God by hospitality, using your home as a haven for the weary, the worn, the poor, the homeless, the traveling servants of Christ, the children in your neighborhood, and their needy parents.

Serve God with your money. God loves a willing spirit. Be as generous with what you have as God Himself has been toward you.

Serve God in the church. Find a useful place there and fill it with distinction. Do not interest yourself in the prominence of your position but in the fruitfulness of your labors.

Serve God by serving humanity.

Serve God by your enthusiasm: "And whatsoever ye do, do it heartily, as to the Lord, and not unto men; Knowing that of the Lord ye shall receive the reward of the inheritance: for ye serve the Lord Christ" (Colossians 3:23-24).

10. Keep moving toward higher ground. When you reach one spiritual goal, immediately set one higher and harder to reach. Steadfastly resist all thoughts of "having arrived"; you have not and will not until you reach the glory. Not for a single moment can you afford to sit back and relax and pretend you have "made it." The goal must be ever before you.

The Apostle Paul, after years of faithful service, after success upon success in his Christian life and ministry, declared, "Brethren, I count not myself to have apprehended: but this one thing I do, forgetting those things which are behind, and reaching forth unto those things which are before, I press toward the mark for the prize of the high calling of God in Christ Jesus" (Philippians 3:13-14).

No matter how long you faithfully walk with Christ, you will still fall short of His glory. After years of diligent service you will still have good reason to yearn to know how to serve Him better. In your lifetime you will never be able to exhaust the Bible, no matter how diligently you study. Your service for Christ will never be complete no matter how sacrificially rendered. Your holiness of heart and life, no matter how earnestly sought, will still fall short of Christ's glory. There will always be new mountains to ascend and new realms of service to explore.

Set lofty goals for yourself. Determine not to linger in the lowlands with the careless masses. Let your spiritual ambition be as great as the Spirit of God can inspire. Press on until you know the very heart of God and then keep right on pressing.

11. Learn to esteem time and regard it as much too precious to waste. The backslider may have plenty of time on his hands to dream and drift, but you do not. Eternity is but a heartbeat away. You are here on a mission. Every moment granted to you has been granted with purpose. If you waste the minutes of this day, it will be easier to waste hours tomorrow. Those who can waste hours are soon comfortable wasting their years. A few short wasted years lead to a wasted life. A wasted life means a wretched eternity.

"See then that ye walk circumspectly, not as fools, but as wise, Redeeming the time, because the days are evil" (Ephesians 5:15,16). Here is God's word for you! Who wastes times? Fools! Who makes the best use of every God-given hour? The wise! Who are the fools? Those who deny God! Who are the wise? Those that know God!

A right relationship with God through Jesus Christ will bring the reclaimed backslider into a right relationship with time. The revived believer sees time as opportunity; the backslider may only see time as a vacuum to be filled. The revived believer regards time as preparation for eternity; the backslider wastes his time and leaves eternity to chance. None of us have any way of knowing how many hours are left us on this earth. They may be many or few, but they are all too precious to lose and none to many in which to complete the work to which God has called us. Use them then for the glory of the God who gives them to you.

12. Consider yourself as Christ considers you—well worth saving. The backslider may be content to treat life with contempt, throwing away time and neglecting opportunities, abusing the body he occupies and scorning the God who made him. In reclaiming you from backsliding, however, God has placed His seal of importance upon you. You mean a great deal to Him. He was not content to leave you where you were. He loves you. He wants you. He has a place of significance for you to occupy. He has brought you back to Himself for a reason. Don't let God's reason be frustrated.

If you consider yourself worthless, you have placed a lower value on your life than Christ does. You meant enough for Him to be willing to pay a great price for your redemption. Despite all your backsliding, He cared enough to keep pursuing you until now you find yourself graciously restored in your relationship with Him. Never lose sight of what your restoration cost Him. Live in the light of the great worth He has placed upon you.

A young person, with little sense of personal worth and no deep realization of his parent's esteem or of the love of God, may easily throw away his life. Turning to drugs or immorality, he testifies to his own sense of worthlessness. But, a youth with a strong realization of the immeasurable worth of his own life, knowing the abiding love of his parents and of God, cannot lightly toss away his life for a few cheap thrills and moments of pleasure.

So it is with the reclaimed backslider. A God-given sense of worth can serve as a great anchor, well cast, in times of severe testing. Let your knowledge of God's great interest in you keep you from backsliding again. Let the awareness that He has reclaimed you for a purpose ever grip you and hold you fast. Jeremiah was moved to write, "The LORD hath appeared of old unto me, saying, Yea, I have loved thee with an everlasting love: therefore with lovingkindness have I drawn thee" (31:3). Here is a word for your soul. God has loved you with an everlasting love; He has drawn you back with lovingkindness. May this assurance keep you always faithful!

Selected
Bibliography

Selected Bibliography

Alexander, Archibald. *The Log College. Biographical Sketches of William Tennent and His students, Together with an Account of the Revivals under Their Ministries.* London: Banner of Truth Trust, 1968. First published in 1851.

Alexander, James Waddell. *The Revival and Its Lessons: a Collection of Fugitive Papers, Having Reference to the Great Awakening, 1858.* New York: American Tract Society, 1858.

Armstrong, Maurice Whitman. *The Great Awakening in Nova Scotia, 1776-1809.* Hartford: American Society of Church History, 1948. A well documented account of a beautiful work of God.

Arthur, William. *Beginnings of a Great Revival, the Awakening in Ulster, Connor.* London: Hamilton, Adams and Co., 1859.

Ashbridge, Thomas. *Why Revival Tarries: God Waits to be Proved.* London: Pickering & Inglis, 1945.

Autrey, C. E. *Revivals of the Old Testament.* Grand Rapids: Zondervan Publishing House, 1960. Studies of eight Old Testament awakenings.

Babson, Roger Ward. *A Revival Is Coming.* New York: Fleming H. Revell Co., 1936. An attempt to show a link between economic decline and spiritual revival and to predict the latter on the basis of the former.

Baillie, John. *Grace Abounding: A Narrative of Facts, Illustrating What the Revival has Done and Is Doing...* London: James Nisbet & Company, 1861. A study of the 1859 awakening in Ireland.

Baker, Ernest. *The Revivals of the Bible.* London: Kingsgate Press, 1906. Scarce but worth reading.

Baker, William. *A Narrative of Remarkable Periods of Success of the Gospel.* Barnstable, England: Printed and sold by J. Avery, 1819.

Baldwin, Thomas. *A Brief Account of the Late Revival of Religion in a Number of Towns in the New-England States.* Boston: Printed & Sold by Manning & Loring, 1799.

————. *A Brief Sketch of the Revival of Religion in Boston in 1803-05.* Boston: Printed by Lincoln & Edmands Company, 1826.

Balmer, Robert. *Address to Elders on the Means To Be Used By Them for Promoting a Revival of Religion.* Berwick, Scotland: Thomas Melrose, 1841.

Bardsley, Cyril Charles Bowman. *Revival: the Need and the Possibilities.* London: Longmans, Green and Co., 1916. A study of some importance.

————. *Studies in Revival.* London: Longmans, Green and Co., 1915. Contributions by several Anglican authors.

Baring-Gould, Sabine. *The Evangelical Revival.* London: Methuen & Co., 1920. A highly biased and critical appraisal.

Barnes, Albert. *The Theory and Desirableness of Revivals, Being Six Sermons.* London: Robert Blackader, 1842. The type of series with which every pastor should favor his congregation.

[Barry, James]. *A Reviving Cordial for a Sin-Sick Despairing Soul, in the Time of Temptation.* London: Printed for the Author, 1699. A splendid treatise on personal revival.

Beardsley, Frank Grenville. *A History of American Revivals.* New York: American Tract Society, 1912. A fairly extensive work.

————. *Religious Progress Through Religious Revivals.* New York: American Tract

Society, 1942. A significant study of the moral, social, political, economic, and religious value of revivals.

Belcher, Joseph. *Two Sermons Preached in Dedham, N. E. The First on a Day Set Apart for Prayer With Fasting, to Implore Spiritual Blessing on the Rising Generation.* Boston: Printed by B. Green, 1710.

Bennett, William Wallace. *A Narrative of the Great Revival which Prevailed in the Southern Armies during the Late Civil War between the States of the Federal Union.* Harrisburg, Va.: Sprinkle Publications, 1976. A reprint of the 1877 edition. A very refreshing work.

Bennett, Willis G. *Pentecost, Its Scope, Power and Perpetuation.* Kansas City, Missouri: Nazarene Publishing House, 1936. A light historical summary of revival movements.

Bickerstaff, Mabel. *Something Wonderful Happened: A Little Book about Revivals for Children.* Llandudno: Committee of the 1904-1905 Revival Memorial Fund, 1954. A fine little volume of the Welsh awakening.

Bingham, Luther Goodyear. *Triumphs of Grace. Fulton Street Prayer Meeting....* New York: Board of Publication of the Reformed Church in New York, 1863.

Bird, Edward. *Some Account of the Great Religious Revival Now Going on in the United States.* London: Seeleys, 1858.

Blackburn, John. *The True Character and Probable Results of American Revivals; a Discourse.* London: Holdsworth and Ball, 1830.

Blair, Samuel. *A Short and Faithful Narrative of the Late Remarkable Revival of Religion in the Congregation of New-Londonderry and Other Parts of Pennsylvania.* Philadelphia: Printed and sold by William Bradford, 1744.

Blair, William Newton. *Gold in Korea.* Topeka, Kansas: H. M. Ives and Sons, 1946. A revision and enlargement of "The Korean Pentecost."

Boles, John B. *The Great Revival, 1787-1805: The Origins of the Southern Evangelical Mind.* Lexington: University Press of Kentucky, 1972. Doubtless the best treatment of this amazing movement.

Bonar, Horatius. *True Revivals and the Men God Uses.* London: The Evangelical Press, n.d. A study of character.

Bowden, Richard. *A Memorial of the Power and Grace of God Manifested in the Recent Awakening and Conversion of Many Persons in the Village and Neighbourhood of Darwen, in the County of Lancaster.* Chelsea, England: Stanhope and Tilling, 1806.

Bradley, Joshua. *Accounts of Religious Revivals in Many Parts of the United States from 1815 to 1818.* Wheaton, Illinois: Richard Owen Roberts, Publishers, 1980. First published in Albany, 1819.

Bready, John Wesley. *England before and after Wesley: The Evangelical Revival and Social Reform.* London: Hodder and Stoughton, 1938. A weak study.

Brock, William. *Revivals, a Lecture Delivered Before the Y. M. C. A. at Ryde.* Ryde: Henry Wayland, 1860. Deals with the Irish awakening of 1859.

Brown, Arthur Douglas. *Revival Addresses.* London: Morgan & Scott, 1922.

Brown, John. *On the Means and Manifestations of a Genuine Revival of Religion: an Address.* Edinburgh: William Oliphant & Son, 1840.

Buell, Samuel. *A Faithful Narrative of the Remarkable Revival of Religion, in the Congregation of East-Hampton, on Long-Island, in the Year of our Lord, 1764. With Some Reflections.* New York: Printed by Samuel Brown, 1766.

Bumstead, John Michael. *The Great Awakening: The Beginnings of Evangelical Pietism in America.* Walthem, Mass.: Blaisdell Publishing Co., 1970. Primary sources in American history.

Burder, Henry Forster. *Pastoral Discourses on Revivals in Religion.* London: Frederick Westley and A. H. Davis, 1829.

Burns, James. *Revivals, Their Laws and Leaders.* London: Hodder and Stoughton, 1909. This volume was reprinted in 1960 by Baker with two additional chapters by Andrew W. Blackwood, Jr. In many ways a good book but weakened by the author's impossible attempt to find laws that govern the mighty acts of God.

Bushman, Richard L. *The Great Awakening: Documents on the Revival of Religion, 1740-1745.* New York: Atheneum, 1970. Extracts from the writings of Solomon Stoddard, Gilbert Tennent, George Whitefield, Eleazer Wheelock, James Davenport, etc.

Cairns, Earle Edwin. *An Endless Line of Splendor: Revivals and Their Leaders from the Great Awakening to the Present.* Wheaton, Illinois: Tyndale House Publishers, 1986. A splendid study, far more accurate and thorough than any to date.

Cameron, Alexander. *The Revival of the Lord's Work Scripturally Considered.* Inverness, Scotland: Gavin Tait, 1864.

Campbell, Duncan. *The Lewis Awakening, 1949-1953.* Edinburgh: The Faith Mission, 1954. On the revival in the Highlands and Islands of Scotland.

————. *The Price and Power of Revival.* Fort Washington: Christian Literature Crusade, 1962 new edition.

Candler, Warren Akin. *Great Revivals and the Great Republic.* Nashville: Publishing House of the M. E. Church, South, 1904. Covers movements from colonial days to D. L. Moody.

Carlberg, Gustav. *China in Revival.* Rock Island, Illinois: Augustana Book Concern, 1936. A comprehensive study of the early twentieth-century movement.

Carson, John T. *God's River in Spate: The Story of the Religious Awakening in Ulster in 1859.* Belfast: Presbyterian Church in Ireland, 1958. An excellent study.

Chambers, Talbot Wilson. *The Noon Prayer Meeting of the North Dutch Church, Fulton Street, New York.* New York: Board of Publishing, Reformed Protestant Dutch Church, 1858. Traces the origins of the 1857-1858 revival.

Chappell, Frederick Leonard. *The Great Awakening of 1740.* Philadelphia: American Baptist Publication Society, 1903.

Charles, Thomas. *Two Letters, Giving an Account of a Revival of Religion in Wales.* Edinburgh: Printed by Hugh Inglis, sold by J. Campbell, 1792,

Church, Pharcellus. *Pentecost: Or the Work of God in Philadelphia, A.D. 1858.* Philadelphia: Parry & M'Millan, 1859.

Cleveland, Catharine Caroline. *The Great Revival in the West.* Chicago: University of Chicago Press, 1916. A Ph.D. thesis.

Coke, Thomas. *An Account of the Great Revival of the Work of God in the City of Dublin, which Commenced on the 4th of July, 1790.* London: Printed in the year 1790.

Coleman, Robert Emerson. *Dry Bones Can Live Again: Revival in the Local Church.* Old-Tappan, New Jersey: Fleming H. Revell Co., 1969.

————. *One Divine Moment.* Old Tappan, New Jersey: Fleming H. Revell, 1970. A first hand report, from the standpoint of a professor, of the revival at Asbury College.

Colman, Benjamin. *The Great God Has Magnified His Word to the Children of Men. A Sermon.* Boston: Printed by T. Fleet for D. Henchman, 1742. A lovely treatment of the Great Awakening by one of its leading participants.

————. *Souls Flying To Jesus Christ Pleasant and Admirable to Behold.* Boston: Printed by G. Rogers, 1740. Another marvelous sermon on the Great Awakening.

Colton, Calvin. *History and Character of American Revivals of Religion, 1733-1832.* London: Westley & Davis, 1832. A scarce but important work. Reprinted by AMS Press in 1973.

Conant, William C. *Narratives of Remarkable Conversions and Revival Incidents.* New York: Derby & Jackson, 1858. A helpful historical summary.

Cooke, William. *The Revival of Religion: the Best Means of Promoting It, and of Securing Its Fruits.* London: Peter & Galpin, 1862.

Cooper, William. *The Sin and Danger of Quenching the Spirit. Two Sermons Preach'd at Portsmouth in the Province of New Hampshire, on December 12th and 19th, 1741. A Time in Which a Remarkable Work of the Spirit of God was Going on in that Place.* Boston: Printed by G. Rogers for S. Eliot, 1741.

Couper, W. J. *Scottish Revivals.* Dundee: James P. Mathew & Co., 1918. Only thirty-seven copies of this inspiring work were printed.

Crawford, Don. *Miracles in Indonesia: God's Power Builds His Church.* Wheaton, Illinois: Tyndale House Publishers, Inc., 1972. On the revival in Indonesia.

Crawford, Mary K. *The Shantung Revival.* Shanghai: China Baptist Publishing Society, 1933. Covers the period from 1930 to 1933.

Cross, Whitney Rogers. *The Burned-Over District: The Social and Intellectual History of Enthusiastic Religion in Western New York, 1800-1850.* Ithaca, New York: Cornell University Press, 1950. An important study of revival movements especially under Jedediah Burchard and Charles G. Finney.

Davenport, Frederick Morgan. *Primitive Traits in Religious Revivals: A Study in Mental and Social Evolution.* New York: Macmillan Co., 1905. A very influential attempt at a sociological explanation of revival phenomena.

Davies, W. Elwyn. *As Eagles Fly: A Study of Revival.* Brooklyn: Bible Christian Union, 1971. A choice little volume.

Davis, George T. B. *When the Fire Fell.* Philadelphia: Million Testament League, 1945. A popular account of several revival movements.

Drummond, Lewis A. *The Awakening That Must Come.* Nashville: Broadman Press, 1978. A Southern Baptist Seminary president's appeal for revival concern.

Edwards, Jonathan. *The Distinguishing Marks of a Work of the Spirit of God.* Boston: S. Kneeland and T. Green, 1741. This often reprinted volume is one of the most important ever published and should be carefully read by every person deeply interested in revival.

————. *A Faithful Narrative of the Surprising Work of God in the Conversion of Many Hundred Souls in Northampton.* London: Printed for John Oswald, 1737. The classic in its field.

————. *An Humble Attempt To Promote Explicit Agreement and Visible Union of God's People In Extraordinary Prayer for the Revival of Religion and the Advancement of Christ's Kingdom on Earth, Pursuant to Scripture-Promises and Prophecies Concerning the Last Time.* Boston: D. Henchman, 1747. A classic call to corporate prayer.

————. *A Treatise Concerning Religious Affections.* Boston: S. Kneeland and T. Green, 1746. The Yale University Press edition of 1959 includes many useful notes.

Ellis, Robert. *Living Echoes of the Welsh Revival, 1904-05.* London: The Delyn Press, n.d. A minor study.

Evans, Eifion. *Revivals: Their Rise, Progress and Achievements.* London, 1960. The annual lecture at the Evangelical Library.

————. *The Welsh Revival of 1904.* Port Talbot, Wales: Evangelical Movement of Wales, n.d. A considerable work.

————. *When He Is Come: An Account of the 1858-60 Revival in Wales.* Bala: Evangelical Movement of Wales, 1959. An excellent study.

Fawcett, Arthur. *The Cambuslang Revival: The Scottish Evangelical Revival of the Eighteenth Century.* London: Banner of Truth Trust, 1971. A much needed study with extensive bibliography.

Fereday, William Wooldreidge. *Josiah and Revival.* Kilmarnock: John Ritchie, Ltd. n.d. A detailed study of an Old Testament revival.

Findlater, John. *The Eternal Springs of Revival.* London: Marshall Brothers, 1914. A review of the unchanging truths which have been most prominent in the great revival movements.

Finney, Charles Grandison. *Lectures on Revivals of Religion.* New York: Leavitt, Lord and Co., 1835. This often reprinted volume is doubtless the most influential book ever published on the subject of revival, but unfortunately it is badly marred by the erroneous viewpoint that a revival is nothing other than the right use of the right means.

Gaustad, Edwin Scott. *The Great Awakening in New England.* New York: Harper & Brothers, 1957. Written as a doctoral thesis.

Gesswein, Armin R. *Is Revival the Normal?* Elizabethtown, Pa.: McBeth Press, 1956. Deals with a very significant question.

Gewehr, Wesley Marsh. *The Great Awakening in Virginia, 1740-1790.* Durham, North Carolina: Duke University Press, 1930. A thesis submitted to the University of Chicago.

Gibson, William. *The Year of Grace: A History of the Ulster Revival of 1859.* Edinburgh: Andrew Elliot, 1860. A highly useful volume although written a little too early in the movement to give a complete picture. This was reprinted in 1943 under the title "More Thrilling than Fiction" in a revised and abbreviated format.

Gih, Andrew. *China's wonderful reviving.* Shanghai: Bethel Mission, n.d.

Gillies, John. *Historical Collections Relating to Remarkable Periods of Success of the Gospel. Reprinted with a preface and Continuation to 1845 by Horatius Bonar.* Edinburgh: Banner of Truth Trust, 1981. A giant volume of primary consequence.

Gillon, Robert Moffatt. *John Davidson of Prestonpans: Reformer, Preacher and Poet in the Generation After Knox.* Edinburgh: James Clarke & Co., 1936. While this volume is not on revival, it does contain a most important chapter on the Revival of the General Assembly of the Church of Scotland in 1596, which grew out of a Solemn Assembly.

Glasgow Revival Tract Society. *Narratives of Revivals of Religion in Scotland, Ireland and Wales.* Glasgow: William Collins, 1830. Brief but delightful sketches on the work at Cambuslang, Kilsyth, Baldernock, Island of Aran, Moulin, Ulster, Island of Lewes, Skye, etc.

Glorious News. A Brief Account of the Late Revivals of Religion in a Number of Towns in the New-England States and Also in Nova Scotia. Philadelphia: S. C. Ustick, 1799.

Goen, Clarence Curtis. *Revivalism and Separatism in New England, 1740-1800.* New Haven: Yale University Press, 1962. A great work with an excellent bibliography.

Goforth, Jonathan. *"By My Spirit."* London: Marshall, Morgan and Scott, n.d. A precious account of revival in China in the early part of the century.

———. *Prevailing Prayer and Revival.* London: China Inland Mission, 1909. An address.

———. *When the Spirit's Fire Swept Korea.* Grand Rapids: Zondervan Publishing House, 1958. On the revival of 1906 and following.

Good News From the Netherlands. Extracts of Letters from Two Ministers in Holland Confirming and Giving Accounts of the Revival of Religion in Guelderland. Boston: Re-printed and sold by S. Kneeland, 1751.

Goodrich, Arthur. *The Story of the Welsh Revival as Told by Eye-witnesses Together with a Sketch of Evan Roberts and His Message to the World.* New York: Fleming G. Revell Co., 1905. With chapters by G. Campbell Morgan, Evan Hopkins, Arthur Goodrich, and others.

Gordon, Marquis Lafayette. *Revivals of Religion. A Paper Read at the Missionary Conference of Osaka, Japan.* Reprinted from the Chinese Recorder, 1885.

Gospel News, Or A Brief Account of the Revival of Religion in Kentucky, and Several Parts of the United States. Likewise Some Pleasing Accounts of the Success and Prospects of the Everlasting Gospel in the East Indies. Baltimore, 1801.

Graham, Samuel L. *Revivals of Religion: A Sermon Preached Before the Synod of North Carolina at Hillsborough, October 16, 1831.* Hillsborough: Printed by Dennis Heart, 1832.

Green, Ashbel. *A Report to the Trustees of the College of New Jersey, Relative to a Revival of Religion Among the Students of Said College, in the Winter and Spring of the Year 1815. With an Appendix. Published by Order of the Trustees.* Philadelphia: Printed for B. B. Hopkins, W. Fay, Printer, 1815.

Green, Samuel. *Times of Refreshing From the Presence of the Lord. A Pastoral Letter to the Church of Christ Meeting at Lion Street, Walworth.* London: Wightman, 1838.

Green, Samuel Gosnell. *Religious Hindrances to Religious Revivals. A Sermon.* London, 1845. The text is I Chronicles 12:32.

————. *Signs of Revival: An Address from the Chair of the Baptist Union, April 27th, 1885.* London, n.d.

Greenfield, John. *Power from on High or the Two Hundredth Anniversary of the Great Moravian Revival, 1727-1927.* Warsaw, Indiana: Published by the author, 1928. History calculated to stir hearts. This work was reprinted in 1967 by Bethany Fellowship under the title "When the Spirit Came."

Griffin, Edward Dorr. *A Letter to the Rev. Ansel D. Eddy, of Canandaigua, New York on the Narrative of the Late Revivals of Religion in the Presbytery of Geneva.* Williamstown, Massachusetts: Printed by Ridley Bannister, 1832. Griffin congragulates Eddy on the stand the Geneva Presbytery took on revivals.

Grubb, Norman Percy. *Continuous Revival.* Philadelphia: Christian Literature Crusade, n.d. Grubb taught that revival is the continuous movement of the Holy Spirit thru the life of the yielded believer, thus following Finney more than the older historic view.

————. *The Price They Paid.* London: Christian Literature Crusade, 19—?

Gwynn, Stephen. *The Ulster Revival: a Strictly Natural and a Strictly Spiritual Work of God, Being a Reply to Certain Popular Opinions, as to Its Supernatural and Physical Character.* Coleraine: S. Eccles, 1859. An important defence of the movement against much popular criticism.

Hall, James. *A Narrative of a Most Extraordinary Work of Religion in North Carolina. Also a Collection of Interesting Letters from James M'Corkle. To Which is Added the Agreeable Intelligence of a Revival in South Carolina.* Philadelphia: Printed and Published by William W. Woodward, 1802.

Hall, William Nelthorpe. *A Narrative of the Origin and Early Progress of the Wonderful Work of God in Laou Ling, Province of Chantung, China....* London: William Cooke, 1867.

Harding, Frederick A. *The Social Impact of the Evangelical Revival.* London: Epworth Press, 1947. Brief but pointed evidence that revivals do more than excite men's emotions.

Harrison, Archibald Harold Walter. *The Evangelical Revival and Christian Reunion.* London: Epworth Press, 1942. Seeks to prove that real church unity can be built upon an evangelical awakening.

Havner, Vance. *Road to Revival.* New York: Fleming H. Revell Co., 1940. Sermons on revival and other subjects.

Heimert, Alan A. *The Great Awakening: Documents Illustrating the Crisis and Its Consequence.* Indianapolis: Bobbs-Merrill Co., 1967. A compilation of useful documents concerning the work of George Whitefield, Jonathan Edwards, etc.

Hession, Roy. *The Calvary Road.* Philadelphia: CLC, 1950. The victorious life is portrayed as the road of continual revival.

Howe, John. *The Prosperous State of the Christian Interest Before the End of Time, By A Plentiful Effusion of the Holy Spirit; Considered in Fifteen Sermons on Ezekiel 39:29. First Preached in 1678.* London: Printed for John Clark & Rich. Hett, 1726.

Hughes, Gwilym. *Evan Roberts, Revivalist. Story of the Liverpool Mission.* Dolgelley, Wales: E. W. Evans, 1905. The record of the three week mission in Liverpool.

Hughes, Philip Edgcumbe. *Revive Us Again.* London: Marshall, Morgan and Scott, 1947. Articles reprinted from "The Life of Faith."

Humphrey, Heman. *Revival Sketches and Manual.* New York: American Tract Society, 1859. Part I consists of sketches of revival movements from apostolic times to the early 19th century. Part II contains the author's views of the way to promote revival.

James, John Angell. *On the Revival of Religion. Address.* London: John Snow, n.d.

Jones, John William. *Christ in the Camp or Religion in Lee's Army.* Richmond, Virginia: B. F. Johnson & Co., 1887. One of the most exciting books ever written on revival.

Jones, Rhys Bevan. *Rent Heavens: The Authentic Story of the Revival of 1904.* Buffalo: European Evangelistic Crusade, 1950. On the movement in Wales.

Kaiser, Walter C., Jr. *Quest for Renewal: Personal Revival in the Old Testament.* Chicago: Moody Press, 1986. Studies in several Old Testament awakenings.

Keller, Charles Roy. *The Second Great Awakening in Connecticut.* New Haven: Yale University Press, 1942. An invaluable study on the early nineteenth-century movement.

Kerr, Matthew. *The Ulster Revival of the 17th Century; an Instructive Chapter in the Early History of Presbyterianism in Ireland.* Belfast: C. Aichson, 1859.

Kirby, Gilbert W. *Revival—Then and Now, 1781-1981.* West Sussex, England, 1981. An historical lecture given at the Whitefield Church in London in celebration of the two-hundredth anniversary of the Countess of Huntingdon's Connexion.

Kirk, Edward Norris. *Lectures on Revivals.* Boston: Congregational Publishing Society, 1875. An excellent series of lectures given at Andover Theological Seminary in 1868.

Knox, Robert. *The Revival in Ireland, Letters from Ministers and Medical Men in Ulster on the Revival of religion in the North of Ireland.* Philadelphia: Wm. S. & Alfred Martien, 1860.

Koch, Kurt E. *Revival Fires in Canada.* Grand Rapids: Kregel Publications, 1973. The incomplete record of a movement which began in Saskatchewan in 1972.

————. *The Revival in Indonesia.* West Germany: Evangelical Publishers, 1972. Sections on Indonesia, Asia in General, and Asbury College.

————. *Victory Through Persecution.* Grand Rapids: Kregel Publications, 1972. On revival in Korea.

————. *Wine of God: Revival in Indonesia, Formosa, Solomon Islands, and South India.* Montreal: Christian Evangelism Publications, 1974.

Lacy, Benjamin Rice. *Revivals in the Midst of the Years.* Richmond, Virginia: John Knox Press, 1943. Lectures delivered at Columbia Theological Seminary in Decatur, Georgia.

Lane, W. W. *The Nature and Means of a Religious Revival. A Sermon.* London: Printed in the Pulpit, 1869.

Lewis, Howell Elvet. *Howell Harris and the Welsh Revivalists.* London: National Council of Evangelical Free Churches, 1911. A volume in the *"Leaders of Revivals"* series.

————. *With Christ Among the Miners: Incidents and Impressions of the Welsh Revival.* London: Hodder and Stoughton, 1906. An important and delightful volume.

Lloyd-Jones, David Martyn. *Revival.* Westchester, Illinois: Crossway Books, 1987. A series of twenty-four sermons preached in commemoration of 1859.

Lockyer, Herbert. *The Mulberry Trees or When Revival Comes.* Grand Rapids: Wm. B. Eerdmans Pub.Co., 1936. Poignant chapters on the need of, steps to, hindrances to and perils of revival.

————. *Revive Us Again!* Oklahoma City, Oklahoma: Western Network Church of the Air, 19--? Messages first delivered on E. F. Webber's Radio Church of the Air.

Lorimer, John Gordon. *Revival: Scriptural and Historical Lectures.* Strathpine North: Covenanter Press, 1977.

Lovejoy, David Sherman. *Religious Enthusiasm and the Great Awakening.* Englewood Cliffs, New Jersey: Prentice-Hall, 1969. A thoughtful study.

Lovelace, Richard F. *Dynamics of Spiritual Life: The Evangelical Theology of Renewal.* Downers Grove: Inter-Varsity Press, 1979.

Lutzer, Erwin Wesley. *Flames of Freedom.* Chicago: Moody Press, 1976. An account of revival in Canada in the 1970's.

McAuley, Thomas. *A Narrative of the Revival of Religion Within the Bounds of the Presbytery of Albany in the Year 1820.* Schenectady: Printed by Isaac Riggs, 1821. Details on Nettleton's powerful ministry.

Macfarlan, Duncan. *The Revivals of the Eighteenth Century, Particularly at Cambuslang. With Three Sermons by the Reverend George Whitefield.* Wheaton, Illinois: Richard Owen Roberts, Publishers, 1980. A reprint of an 1847 work.

MacRae, Alexander. *Revivals in the Highlands and Islands in the 19th Century.* Stirling,

Scotland: E. Mackay, 1905. A revealing work.

Matthews, David. *I Saw the Welsh Revival.* Chicago: Moody Press, 1951. A firsthand report of 1904-1905.

Maxson, Charles Hartshorn. *The Great Awakening in the Middle Colonies.* Chicago: University of Chicago Press, 1920. A thoroughly documented work.

Ministers of the Church of Scotland. *Lectures on the Revival of Religion.* Wheaton, Illinois: Richard Owen Roberts, Publishers, 1980. First published in 1840. One of the most useful volumes ever published.

Modersohn, Ernst. *Men of Revival in Germany.* Frankfurt/Main: Harold Publishers, n.d. Brief biographies of German revival leaders.

Moore, Martin. *Boston Revival, 1842. A Brief History of the Evangelical Churches of Boston Together with a More Particular Account of the Revival of 1842.* Wheaton, Illinois: Richard Owen Roberts, Publishers, 1980. A reprint of the 1842 edition. This volume focuses on the work of Elder Jacob Knapp.

Morgan, George Campbell. *The Source and Power of the Welsh Revival.* Boston: Pilgrim Press, n.d. First published in the London "Christian Commonwealth."

Morgan, John James. *The '59 Revival in Wales: Some Incidents in the Life and Work of David Morgan.* Mold, Wales: J. J. Morgan, 1909. A very important study.

Morgan, John Vyrnwy. *The Welsh Religious Revival, 1904-1905. A retrospect and a Criticism.* London: Chapman and Hall, 1909. A highly critical but thought-provoking volume.

Morton, Daniel Oliver. *A Narrative of a Revival of Religion in Springfield, Vermont.* Springfield: n.p., 1834.

Murray, Iain H. *The Puritan Hope: A Study in Revival and the Interpretation of Prophecy.* London: The Banner of Truth Trust, 1971. A very great work.

Myles, William. *Scriptural Marks of a Revival of the Work of God. A Sermon.* Rochdale, England, 1799. A sermon on Zechariah 8:21.

Narrative of the Surprising Work of God in the Conversion of Souls in Kilsyth, Finnieston, and Cumerrauld, and the Revival of Religion in Anderston and Paisley; with an Account of the Remarkable Occurrences Which Took Place at the Dispensation of the Sacrament at Kilsyth, on 22nd September, 1839. Glasgow: David Maclure, 1839.

Newell, Philip R. *Revival on God's Terms: A Consideration of Scriptural Conditions which God Waits for His People to Fulfill.* Chicago: Moody Press, n.d. An exposition of 2 Chronicles 7:14.

Nissenbaum, Stephen. *The Great Awakening at Yale College.* Belmont, California: Wadsworth Publishing Co., 1972. A critical work.

Noble, William Francis Pringle. *A Century of Gospel Work: 1776-1876.* Philadelphia: H. C. Watts & Co., 1876. A large and detailed volume containing descriptions of the revivals and sketches of the leaders.

Ockenga, Harold John. *The Great Awakening: the Story of the Marvelous Revival under the Ministry of Rev. George Whitefield. May We Expect Another Great Awakening in 1940?* Boston: Fellowship Press, 1940. A bicentenary publication.

Old South Chapel Prayer Meetings: Its Origin and History. Boston: J. E. Tilton & Co., 1859. A record of the Boston Revival of 1858-1859.

Olford, Stephen Frederick. *Heart-Cry for Revival: Expository Sermons on Revival.* Westwood, N.J.: Fleming H. Revell Co., 1962. Messages delivered at Calvary Baptist Church in New York City.

Orr, James Edwin. *Campus Aflame: Dynamics of Student Religious Revolution.* Glendale: Regal Books, 1972. Evangelical awakenings in collegiate communities.

————. *The Church Must First Repent: Chapters on Revival.* London: Marshall, Morgan & Scott, 1937. A clear call to revival.

————. *The Eager Feet: Evangelical Awakenings, 1790-1830.* Chicago: Moody Press, 1975.

————. *Evangelical Awakenings in Africa.* Minneapolis: Bethany Fellowship, 1975.

————. *Evangelical Awakenings in Eastern Asia.* Minneapolis: Bethany Fellowship, 1975.

————. *Evangelical Awakenings in Latin America.* Minneapolis: Bethany Fellowship, 1978.

————. *Evangelical Awakenings in Southern Asia.* Minneapolis: Bethany Fellowship, 1975.

————. *Evangelical Awakenings in the South Seas.* Minneapolis: Bethany Fellowship, 1976.

————. *The Event of the Century: the 1857-1858 Awakening.* Edited by Richard Owen Roberts. Wheaton, Illinois: International Awakening Press, 1989.

————. *The Fervent Prayer: The Worldwide Impact of the Great Awakening of 1858.* Chicago: Moody Press, 1974.

————. *The Flaming Tongue: The Impact of the Twentieth Century Revivals.* Chicago: Moody Press, 1973.

————. *The Light of the Nations: Evangelical Renewal and Advance in the Nineteenth Century.* Grand Rapids: Eerdmans, 1965.

————. *My All, His All.* Edited by Richard Owen Roberts. Wheaton, Illinois: International Awakening Press, 1989. An excellent work on personal renewal.

————. *The Second Evangelical Awakening in America.* London: Marshall, Morgan & Scott, 1952.

————. *The Second Evangelical Awakening in Britain.* London: Marshall, Morgan & Scott, 1949.

Overton, John Henry. *The Evangelical Revival in the Eighteenth Century.* London: Longmans, Green & Co., 1886. A popular but useful account.

Paisley, Ian R. K. *The "Fifty-Nine" Revival: An Authentic History of the Great Ulster Awakening of 1859.* Belfast: The Free Presbyterian Church of Ulster, 1958. Warm and vital.

Penn-Lewis, Mrs. Jesse. *The Awakening in Wales and Some of the Hidden Springs.* London: Marshall Brothers, 1905. Includes many valuable insights.

————. *War on the Saints: A Text Book on the Work of Deceiving Spirits among the Children of God, and the Way of Deliverance. Written in Collaboration with Evan Roberts.* Leicester: The "Overcomer" Book Room, 1922. In certain respects this volume seems to seek to correct some of the prominent errors in the 1904-05 awakening in Wales. Unfortunately, we are unable, at this late date, to be sure of the part Mr. Roberts played in the writing of the volume. When securing this book, be sure to avoid the more recent abridged editions which are most unsatisfactory.

Peters, George W. *Indonesia Revival: Facts on Timor.* Grand Rapids: Zondervan, 1973. A careful sorting out of the truth from the fabrications certain other books on this revival feature.

Phillips, Daniel M. *Evan Roberts, the Great Welsh Revivalist and His Work.* London: Marshall Brothers, 1906. A massive volume.

Phillips, Thomas. *The Welsh Revival: Its Origin and Development.* London: James Nisbet & Co., 1860. On the 1858-59 movement.

Plowman, Edward E. *The Jesus Movement in America.* New York: Pyramid Books, 1971. A popular account of an unusual movement.

Porter, Ebenezer. *Letters on the Religious Revival which Prevailed about the Beginning of the Present Century.* Boston: Congregational Board of Publications, 1858. The letters were addressed to the students who were part of the Revival Association at Andover Theological Seminary.

Presbyterian Board of Publications. *Narratives of Revivals of Religion in Scotland, Ireland, Wales and America.* Philadelphia: 1855. A delightful volume.

Prime, Samuel Irenaeus. *Five Years of Prayer, With the Answers.* New York: Harper & Brothers, 1864. A sequel.

————. *The Power of Prayer Illustrated in the Wonderful Displays of Divine Grace at the Fulton Street and Other Meetings in New York and Elsewhere.* New York: Sheldon, Blakeman & Co., 1859. Two great works on the 1857 movement.

Prince, Thomas. *The Christian History Containing Accounts of the Revival and*

Propagation of Religion in Great Britain and America for the Years 1743, 1744. Boston: S. Kneeland and T. Green, 1744, 1745. 2 volumes. Originally published each Saturday, the two volumes contain 104 accounts.

Ravenhill, Leonard. *Revival Praying.* Minneapolis: Bethany Fellowship, 1962. An earnest call to the kind of praying God hears.

————. *Why Revival Tarries.* Minneapolis: Bethany Fellowship, 1959. The follies of the Church and her leaders are laid bare in this careful treatment of the hindrances to real revival.

Reed, Andrew. *A Narrative of the Visit to the American Churches, by the Deputation from the Congregational Union of England and Wales.* New York: Harper & Bros., 1835. 2 volumes. Firsthand observations on revivals and camp meetings.

————. *The Revival of Religion, a Narrative of the State of Religion at Wycliffe Chapel during the year 1839.* London: Thomas Ward & Co., 1840.

Reid, William. *Authentic Records of Revival, Now in Progress in the United Kingdom.* Wheaton, Illinois: Richard Owen Roberts, Publishers, 1980. An introduction by Horatius Bonar deals with modern hostilities to revivals. This is a reprint of the 1860 edition.

Reminiscences of the Revival of '59 and the Sixties. Aberdeen, Scotland: The University Press, 1910. Appreciations and brief biographies of some of the leaders.

Rendall, Ted S. *Fire in the Church.* Chicago: Moody Press, 1974. An urgent call to revival.

Rice, David. *A Sermon on the Present Revival of Religion, etc. in this Country. Preached at the Opening of the Kentucky Synod.* Lexington: Printed by Joseph Charless, 1803.

Robe, James. *The Christian Monthly History; Or an Account of the Revival and Progress of Religion, Abroad and at Home, November 1743-January, 1746.* Edinburgh: R. Fleming and A. Allison, 1743-1746. 2 volumes. Very important, but rare.

Roberts, Emry. *Revival and Its Fruits,* by Emry Roberts; and *The Revival of 1762* and *William Williams of Pantycelyn* by R. Geraint Gruffydd. The Evangelical Library of Wales, 1981. Two lectures.

Roberts, R. Phillip. *Continuity and Change: London Calvinistic Baptists and the Evangelical Revival, 1760-1820.* Wheaton, Illinois: Richard Owen Roberts, Publishers, 1989. A Ph.D. thesis submitted to the Free University of Amsterdam, 1989.

Roberts, Richard Owen, editor. *Glory Filled the Land: a trilogy on the Welsh Revival, 1904-1905.* By H. Elvet Lewis, G. Campbell Morgan, I. V. Neprash. Wheaton, Illinois: International Awakening Press, 1989.

————. *Lord, I Agree: Twelve Articles of Explicit Agreement Between the Covenant Keeping God and the Reviving Believer.* Wheaton, Illinois: International Awakening Press, 1990.

————. *Revival Literature: an Annotated Bibliography with Biographical and Historical Notices.* Wheaton, Illinois: Richard Owen Roberts, Publishers, 1987. Provides full bibliographical details on more than 6,000 volumes pertaining to revival.

————. *The Solemn Assembly.* Wheaton, Illinois: International Awakening Press, 1989. The divinely instituted answer to the problem of corporate sin.

————. *Whitefield In Print: a Bibliographic Record of Works By, For, and Against George Whitefield with annotations, Biographical and Historical Notices, and Bibliographies of His Associates and Contemporaries. The Whole Forming a Literary History of the Great Eighteenth Century Revival.* Wheaton, Illinois: Richard Owen Roberts, Publishers, 1988. Full bibliographic details on more than 8,000 volumes.

Sangster, William Edwin. *Revival: The Need and the Way.* London: Epworth Press, 1957. An encouraging word from a great Methodist preacher.

[Seccombe, Joseph]. *Some Occasional Thoughts on the Influence of the Spirit. With Seasonable Cautions Against Mistakes and Abuses.* Boston: Printed and sold by S. Kneeland and T. Green, 1742.

Sewall, Joseph. *God's People Must Enquire of Him to Bestow the Blessings Promised in His Word. A sermon... on a Day of Prayer Observed by the South Church and*

Congregation in Boston, to Seek of God the More Plentiful Effusion of His Holy Spirit upon Them and His People. Boston: Printed by D. Fowle, 1742. A model sermon, the likes of which should be preached in every church throughout the land.

Shoemaker, Samuel Moor. *Revive Thy Church Beginning With Me.* New York: Harper and Brothers, 1948. A "how to" book.

Simpson, R. T. *Recollections of and Reflections on the Revival of 1859, with Notes and Additions.* Dungannon: Tyrone Printing Company, 1909.

Smith, Oswald J. *The Revival We Need.* New York: Christian Alliance Publishing Co., 1925. Poignant appeals for burdened hearts.

Smith, R. S. *Recollections of Nettleton and the Great Revival of 1820.* Albany, New York, 1848. A wonderful account with emphasis on the work at Union College in Schenectady, New York.

Smith, Timothy Lawrence. *Revivalism and Social Reform in Mid-Nineteenth Century America.* Nashville: Abingdon Press, 1957. A warmly sympathetic and carefully documented work.

Smith, Wilbur Moorehead. *The Glorious Revival Under Hezekiah.* Grand Rapids: Zondervan Publishing House, 1937. A poignant study.

Sprague, William Buell. *Lectures on Revivals of Religion.* London: Banner of Truth Trust, 1959. A reprint of Sprague's nine lectures with an appendix of letters on revival from twenty leading American clergymen. A splendid book.

Spurgeon, Charles Haddon. *C. H. Spurgeon's Sermons on Revival. Selected and Edited by Rev. Dr. Charles T. Cook.* Grand Rapids: Zondervan Pub. House, 1958.

————. *Revival Year Sermons Preached at the Surrey Gardens Music Hall During 1859.* London: The Banner of Truth Trust, 1959. Includes a brief and pithy introduction by the publishers.

————. *The Story of God's Mighty Acts.* London: Evangelical Press, n.d. A sermon on the revival of 1859 preached in the Surrey Gardens Music Hall, Sunday, July 17, 1859.

————. *Twelve Revival Sermons.* New York: Fleming H. Revell Company, 18--? Excellent textual sermons.

Stewart, James Alexander. *Invasion of Wales By the Spirit Through Evan Roberts.* Fort Washington: CLC, 1963. Stewart was well acquainted with Roberts' family.

————. *Opened Windows.* London: Marshall, Morgan and Scott, 1958. An exposition of the methods and message Stewart used in his revival work.

Stopford, Edward Adderley. *The Work and the Counterwork; or, the Religious Revival in Belfast. With an Explanation of the Physical Phenomena.* Dublin: Hodges, Smith & Co., 1859.

Sweet, William Warren. *Revivalism in America, Its Origins, Growth, and Decline.* New York: Charles Scribner's Sons, 1944. A respected historian's interpretation.

Tari, Mel. *The Gentle Breeze.* Carol Stream, Illinois: Creation House, 1974. A further account of the Indonesian revival.

————. *Like a Mighty Wind.* Carol Stream, Illinois: Creation House, 1972. The accuracy of Tari's works is seriously questioned by thoughtful Christians.

Tarr, Charles R. *A New Wind Blowing.* Anderson, Indiana: Warner Press, 1972. Story of revival in Anderson.

Tatford, Frederick Albert. *Revival in Our Time.* London: The Paternoster Press, 1947. Addresses given at Westminster Chapel by several choice servants of Christ.

Taylor, William. *An Account of a Revival of Religion in Jerusalem With Observations on Some of the Most Remarkable Things that Took Place in the Work; Or, A Sermon Delivered at Chester, New Hampshire.* Concord: Printed by J. B. Moore, 1823.

Tennent, Gilbert. *A Funeral Sermon Occasion'd By the Death of the Rev. Mr. John Rowland, Who Departed This Life, April the 12th, 1745.* Philadelphia: William Bradford, 1745. This volume also contains: *A Narrative of the Revival and Progress of Religion in the Towns of Hopewell, Amwell and Maiden-head, in New Jersey, and New Providence in Pennsylvania.* By John Rowland.

Thacher, Thomas. *A Fast of God's Choosing, Plainly Opened, for the Help of Those*

Poor in Spirit, Whose Hearts are Set to Seek the Lord Their God In New-England. Boston: Printed by John Foster, 1678. A Solemn Assembly sermon of great consequence.

Thomas, Isaac David Ellis. *God's Harvest.* Bala, Wales: Evangelical Press of Wales, n.d. A delightful little study on the 1904-1905 awakening.

Thompson, Charles Lemuel. *Times of Refreshing: A History of American Revivals from, 1740 to 1877, with their Philosophy and Methods.* Chicago: L. T. Palmer & Co., 1866. A popular work.

Thornbury, John F. *God Sent Revival: the Story of Asahel Nettleton and the Second Great Awakening.* Welwyn, Herts: Evangelical Press, 1977.

Times of Refreshing; Being Notices of Some of the Religious Awakenings Which Have Taken Place in the United Kingdom, With Special Reference to the Revival in Aberdeen. Aberdeen, Scotland: George and Robert King, 1859.

Townsend, Luther Tracy. *The Supernatural Factors in Religious Revivals.* Boston: Lee and Shepard, 1877. A comparison of Moody and Sankey with George Whitefield.

Tracy, Joseph. *The Great Awakening: a History of the Revival of Religion in the Times of Edwards and Whitefield.* Edinburgh: Banner of Truth Trust, 1976. Reprinted from the 1842 edition of a great classic.

Tyler, Bennet. *New England Revivals, As They Existed at the Close of the Eighteenth and the Beginning of the Nineteenth Centuries.* Wheaton, Illinois: Richard Owen Roberts, Publishers, 1980. This delightful volume was reprinted from the 1846 Boston edition.

Wadsworth, Ernest M. *What Will Bring Revival?* Philadelphia: The Sunday School Times Co., 1945. Ten brief studies.

————. *Will Revival Come?* Chicago: Great Commission Prayer League, 1936. A series of brief articles.

Wallis, Arthur. *In the Day of Thy Power: The Spiritual Principles of Revival.* London: Christian Literature Crusade, 1956. A study of the biblical grounds for revival and of the conditions that still must be met.

Warren, Max. *Revival: An Enquiry.* London: SCM Press, 1954. An important appraisal of the East African revival which began about 1937.

Watt, Eva Stuart. *Floods on Dry Ground: Revival in the Congo.* London: Marshall, Morgan and Scott, 1939. A useful record of the movement which began in 1920.

Webster, James. *The Revival in Manchuria.* London: Marshall, Morgan and Scott, 1910. A little known movement.

Weir, John. *Irish Revivals. The Ulster Awakening: Its Origin, Progress and Fruit.* London: Arthur Hall, Virtue & Co., 1860.

Weisberger, Bernard A. *They Gathered at the River: The Story of the Great Revivalists and Their Impact Upon Religion in America.* Boston: Little, Brown and Co., 1958. The author sums up his work nicely in saying, "This is a book about religion, and not a religious book."

Westgarth, J. W. *The Holy Spirit and the Primitive Mind: A Remarkable Account of a Spiritual Awakening in Darkest Africa.* London: Victory Press, 1946. On the 1927 awakening.

Wigglesworth, Samuel. *An Essay For Reviving Religion, a Sermon.* Boston: S. Kneeland, 1733. On Habakkuk 3:2.

Wight, Fred Hartley. *If My People: Repentance and Revival.* Butler, Indiana: The Highley Press, 1959. A crucial issue is carefully treated in this important study.

Williams, William. *The Experience Meeting: An Introduction to the Welsh Societies of the Evangelical Awakening.* This book was translated by Mrs. Lloyd-Jones and includes an introduction by Dr. D. Martyn Lloyd-Jones. London: The Evangelical Press, 1973. Williams was the great song-writer of the revival in Wales.

Willis, Avery T., Jr. *Indonesian Revival: Why Two Million Came to Christ.* Pasadena, California: William Carey Library, 1977.

Williston, Seth. *A Sermon on Revivals of Religion: Containing a Caution to the Church, in the Nineteenth Century, to Beware of the Devices of Satan in Corrupting Them.*

New York: D. Fanshaw, 1827.

Winslow, Octavius. *Personal Declension and Revival of Religion in the Soul.* London: Banner of Truth Trust. A reprint of the 1841 edition.

Wood, Arthur Skevington. *And With Fire: Messages on Revival.* London: Pickering and Inglis, 1958. Bible expositions.

————. *The Inextinguishable Blaze: Spiritual Renewal and Advance in the Eighteenth Century.* London: Paternoster Press, 1960. A fresh and vital study of the Evangelical Awakening.

Woodbridge, John. *Revivals: or, the Appropriate Means of Promoting True Religion. A Sermon.* Bridgeport, Connecticut: Standard Office, 1841.

Woodward, William Wallis. *Surprising Accounts of the Revival of Religion in the United States of America, in Different Parts of the World, and Among Different Denominations of Christians.* Philadelphia: Printed & Published by William W. Woodward, 1802.

Yates, William. *The Outpouring of the Holy Spirit Essential to a Revival of Religion; a Sermon.* Gloucester: W. Verrinder, 1829.

Young, Robert. *The Importance of Prayer-Meetings in Promoting the Revival of Religion.* New York: G. Lane and P. P. Sandford, 1841.